...ueblo Peoples
on the
Pajarito Plateau

Pueblo Peoples

on the

Pajarito Plateau

ARCHAEOLOGY AND EFFICIENCY

David E. Stuart

University of New Mexico Press

Albuquerque

Published 2010 in the United States of America
14   13   12   11   10   1   2   3   4   5

LIBRARY OF CONGRESS CATALOGING-IN-PUBLICATION DATA
Stuart, David E.
Pueblo peoples on the Pajarito Plateau: archaeology and efficiency/
    David E. Stuart.
      p. cm.
Includes bibliographical references and index.

ISBN 978-0-8263-4911-8 (paper: alk. paper)

 1. Pueblo Indians—New Mexico—Pajarito Plateau—Antiquities.
 2. Pueblo Indians—New Mexico—Bandelier National
    Monument—Antiquities.
 3. Social archaeology—New Mexico—Pajarito Plateau.
 4. Social archaeology—New Mexico—Bandelier National Monument.
 5. Survival skills—New Mexico—Pajarito Plateau—History—To 1500.
 6. Survival skills—New Mexico—Bandelier National Monument—
    History—To 1500.
 7. Pueblo Indians—New Mexico—Pajarito Plateau—Social life and customs.
 8. Pueblo Indians—New Mexico—Bandelier National Monument—
    Social life and customs.
 9. Pajarito Plateau (N.M.)—Antiquities. 10. Bandelier National Monument
    (N.M.)—Antiquities.
 I. Title.

E99.P9S86 2010
978.9004'974—dc22
                              2010027469

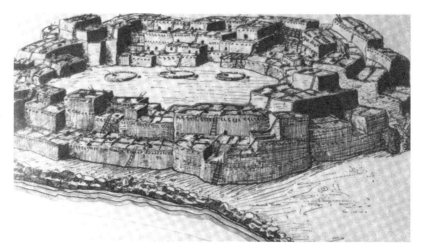

Artist's conception of the pueblo called Tyuonyi at Bandelier National Monument.
This rendition makes the building look more massive than it probably was.
Courtesy National Park Service, Bandelier National Monument.

Contents

Preface

Since my book *The Magic of Bandelier* was published in 1989, the raw archaeological data available from New Mexico's Bandelier National Monument have tripled. Archaeologists such as Robert Powers, Janet Orcutt, Timothy Kohler, and Rory Gauthier are to thank for this bounty. Because of their work, this book is not just a freshening up of the earlier one. It is so heavily rewritten, added to, and refocused that it isn't the same book at all.

I wrote *The Magic of Bandelier* as a guidebook for visitors at a time when far fewer guidebooks existed than is now the case (although Dorothy Hoard's several editions remain mandatory reading). In 2005, the School for Advanced Research Press in Santa Fe, New Mexico, published *The Peopling of Bandelier*, edited by Robert Powers, which filled the need for a book painting a much larger picture of Bandelier than those available in marker-by-marker trail guides. That well-written, beautifully illustrated, and information-rich book offers readers a wide-angle view of anthropological archaeology at work.

I have a more precise goal for *Pueblo Peoples on the Pajarito Plateau*. Here I concentrate on settlement and subsistence data in order to show how Bandelier Monument and the plateau on which it sits became the Southwest's most densely populated area after the powerful society centered in Chaco Canyon, New Mexico, collapsed in the 1100s CE ("common era"). Until then only lightly inhabited by foraging and hunting folk, the Pajarito Plateau had remained probably the northern Southwest's most important upland ecological preserve. Migrating to it gave some of the stunned survivors of Chaco's fall a place in which to refashion themselves and rise from catastrophe. This re-formation of ancestral Pueblo society required people to rebalance the Chacoans' final obsession with growth, grandeur, and hierarchy with a return to a way of life of much greater efficiency, moderation, and practicality. These qualities were key to their survival.

In another earlier book, *Anasazi America* (2000), I wrote about forces I refer to as "power" and "efficiency" in human social evolution. Briefly, power is most valuable for pushing growth and managing hostile competitors as a society enlarges. Its most notable archaeological signature is huge structures and a costly, expanding infrastructure. Efficiency reigns in times of want or scarcity, so its archaeological signature is a modest, practical infrastructure, fewer lavish structures, and tools and other goods that are used, repaired, and reused. Getting the balance between power and efficiency right for the technology and resources available at a given time is the most critical issue a society faces. Fantasy and wishful thinking do not suffice.

The story I tell about Bandelier and the northern Rio Grande region differs a bit from that offered by Powers and his coauthors in *The Peopling of Bandelier* and from the view put forward by Timothy Kohler in his book *Archaeology of Bandelier National Monument* (2004). They argued that Bandelier began to fill up with people about 1150, and thereafter population shifted into higher elevations. I believe that a few farming-focused early-comers began to filter into the northern Rio Grande as early as the 1000s, digging pithouses and founding small pueblos. A peak of pithouse construction at higher elevations to the north of Bandelier can be dated to 1153 on the basis of patterns across 200,000 square miles of the greater Southwest. Just why similar pithouses have not been found in the monument itself is a significant question. Was the Pajarito still inhabited by Archaic-style forager-hunters long after they disappeared from the Four Corners country? Or was most of the southern Pajarito a hunting preserve so valuable to surrounding, long-established, upland pithouse dwellers that few actually lived in it? Examples of such hunting grounds are certainly known for many historic tribal societies.

I deviate again from earlier writers' formulations of the years from 1290 to 1325 by arguing that because of drought, the main body of the upland populations moved eastward—downhill and downstream—into the Rio Grande Valley at that time. Some villagers then revisited their briefly abandoned upland holdings as early as the 1320s to 1340s, using the higher elevations as a safety valve during dry periods when farming in the valley bottom became too unreliable.

These departures arise from the fact that I am a student not of pottery or architectural form but of evolutionary and ecological dynamics as evidenced in broad settlement patterns and people's uses of different niches in the landscape. Thus, I see the beginning and the first, temporary, end-ing of the Pajarito's so-called Coalition period—the years between about 1290 and 1325—as dynamically critical to understanding the re-formation of Puebloan society, a renewal that allowed it to survive for another eight hundred years.

This volume indulges my passion for guiding readers toward an under-standing of just how Bandelier National Monument and the Pajarito Plateau fit into an epic Southwestern story, now six hundred human generations long. Although I focus on the archaeology of the monument and the pla-teau, much of what archaeologists know about them depends on events that happened to ancient people far away and centuries before the sites preserved in the monument were built. Learning about this context is the best way to make good sense of the archaeological remains found on the plateau.

In an age when America's politics, economics, and "evening news" are often dealt with simplistically, I believe the nuances of context, in both modern daily life and archaeology, matter. In that sense, the story of the ancient Pajarito Plateau is an elegant reminder that there were—and are—no shortcuts to cultural survival.

Acknowledgments

I am grateful to Mary Powell and Marta Weigle of Ancient City Press for taking pains in 1989 to produce *The Magic of Bandelier*, from which I borrowed some material, now much altered, for this book. The current edition has benefited greatly from the skills of the University of New Mexico Press's editorial and design team, including Luther Wilson, Elizabeth Hadas, Elise McHugh, Elizabeth Albright, and Cheryl Carrington. I am also grateful that the press agreed to assign the editing of the book to Jane Kepp, who has a rare talent for making writing clear and vibrant. I think of her as the master diamond cutter of anthropological texts—she knows which material must be cut and which polished in order to bring out the color and clarity of the words.

I thank Tom Baker of Baker Aerial Archaeology for his stunning aerial photographs, Michael P. Marshall for the use of his photographic library of ceramic artifacts, and Richard Pfaff for his cover and frontispiece photographs. I also thank Rory P. Gauthier, archaeologist at Bandelier National Monument, who urged me to set aside other book projects in order to prepare this text for another generation of visitors to Bandelier. Rory is more knowledgeable than I about many recent finds in the monument, so I relied on him to read drafts, check facts, and nudge me back on course when my love of large overviews carried me afield. He provided up-to-the-month survey data through 2009, and his colleague Jamie Civitello prepared wonderful site distribution maps (see figures on pages 90 and 109) that appear in print here for the first time.

PART ONE

Bandelier
National Monument

Aerial view of Valles Caldera, the collapsed bowl of an ancient volcano, in the Jemez Mountains just west of Bandelier National Monument. The distant snow line is on the Sangre de Cristo Mountains to the east and north, across the Rio Grande Valley. Courtesy National Park Service, Bandelier National Monument, 1964.

Frijoles Creek in winter. Tyuonyi is to the right, out of view. Courtesy National Park Service, Bandelier National Monument, 1978.

Juniper Campground

July 5, 1986, 8:00 p.m.

T he crowd gathers slowly. By twos and threes they file into the huge, darkening amphitheater at Juniper Campground. There, a mile and one-third above sea level, the night sky is breathtaking. Brilliant stars and the Milky Way's swirling arc of cloudy light mingle with recorded flute music composed more than a thousand years ago.

This is Bandelier National Monument, in the heart of northern New Mexico's Pajarito Plateau—fascinating by day, a natural theater by night. The crowd at Juniper Campground is hushed. Some people turn to watch flashlights flickering along nearby paths as latecomers arrive from surrounding campgrounds. Children snuggle under blankets, quietly awaiting the promised Friday night campfire lecture. British accents carry softly from the second row of wooden bleachers. To the right there is a friendly twang, typical of East Texas or Louisiana. Connecticut's clipped vowels are out there, too, hidden in the dark. One boy in the front row, who wears his baseball cap sideways, gapes in awe as Sari Stein lights a bonfire at the amphitheater's edge, then comes to sit in the front row with her tape recorder. In the summer months she arranges speakers' programs for the monument. Tonight the topic is a regional favorite—"New Mexico's Archaeological Heritage."

As the flute music stops, the rustic stone stage is lit and Rory Gauthier, a ranger at the monument, steps up to introduce a local archaeologist brought in to lecture. Rory brings the hushed crowd back to earth with some anecdotes, welcomes them to Bandelier, and gives them a brief background to the scheduled lecture. He neglects to mention that he has coauthored a substantial college text on Southwestern archaeology, was born and raised in nearby Los Alamos, New Mexico, and knows more about the archaeology of the surrounding area than all but a few other living scholars. Rory is modest.

Next comes the story of ancient Bandelier. The earliest villages there were built by descendants of the ancestral Pueblo people of Chaco Canyon and its surroundings, more than fifty miles to the west. (Anthropologists once called the early Puebloan peoples "Anasazi," a Navajo word best translated as

The remains of Tyuonyi in Frijoles Canyon. © Baker Aerial Archaeology—
Tom Baker, 2007.

"ancestors of our enemies," but contemporary Pueblo Indians prefer not
to see it used.) The Chaco people abandoned their basin-land towns about
eight hundred years ago. In the 1100s CE ("common era," the equivalent of
AD), drought in the Chaco country brought a trickle of displaced western
New Mexico farmers into the cool, forested highlands of the Pajarito Plateau, where rainfall is greater than in the lowlands and where deep winter
snow nourishes crystal-clear streams in nearly every canyon. Years later the
trickle of immigrants became a wave. Bandelier's earliest stone masonry
pueblos, built in the late 1100s, were numerous, although small and widely
scattered. But even in this new home, times were hard for the immigrants
because cold nighttime temperatures prevented them from harvesting the
large-cobbed corn they had grown during the earlier Chacoan era. Rectangular, sandstone-slabbed bins in which they roasted green corn at high elevation compensated to a degree. Still, villagers suffered recurring hunger.

In the early thirteenth century, Bandelier's Indian people gathered into
the first large cliff dwellings to be built there, abandoning some of their
earlier small, mesa-top farming hamlets. Throughout the 1200s, Bandelier's
canyons filled with south-facing cliff dwellings designed to capture warmth
efficiently from the low winter sun. The back rooms of these pueblos were

often cut into the soft volcanic tuff of the mesas, overlooking sparkling creeks. Above the monument's contemporary headquarters, cave rooms lined the main wall of Frijoles Canyon. Long rows of fist-sized socket holes, which once supported the roof beams (*vigas*) of stone masonry dwelling rooms, show where those rooms projected outward from the cliff face, in front of the cave rooms.

In the late 1200s, a dependable water supply became of utmost importance to the monument's inhabitants. Because Frijoles Creek ran year-round, its canyon was a perfect place for a larger village. There, the great circular structure of Tyuonyi (Qu-weh-nee, in the Keres Pueblo language) grew until it was two or three stories tall and contained more than four hundred rooms. Founded just before 1300, it prospered episodically into the early 1500s and then was abandoned. By then Pueblo people had concentrated their largest settlements along the Rio Grande Valley, a few miles to the east. Descendants of the Tyuonyi people—speakers of the Keres language—still inhabit the Rio Grande pueblos of Cochiti, Santo Domingo, and San Felipe.

As the lecture ends, a young woman asks what eventually became of the people who inhabited the ruined villages all around. The lecturer tells her that droughts and overcrowding in the fragile canyon ecosystem may have caused a significant portion of Bandelier's ancient population to move down into the Rio Grande Valley or to perish during the two difficult centuries between 1100 and 1300 CE. The story of New Mexico's Pueblo heritage is one of pain and hardship—but also one of ingenuity, faith, and hope, all keys to the triumph of Pueblo Indian survival.

After more questions, the crowd drifts away, flashlights twinkling. Later, a meteor shower explodes above the starlit north rim of Frijoles Canyon. Below, the night breeze wanders gently among great ponderosa pines while Frijoles Creek bubbles down to the Rio Grande. By dawn its passing waters will have given yet another day's precious life to someone's cornfields.

The Character of Ancient Places

The American Southwest abounds with traces of the homes of people who lived there for thousands of years before the first white colonists arrived. A few of the larger and more spectacular ruined villages have become well-known as national parks and monuments, and Bandelier National Monument is a special one. Today these ruined buildings may strike visitors as silent piles of clay and stone, but each is important as a unique chapter in the story of pre-Columbian society in America. And each conveys a special personality, forged from its geographical setting and from a lingering sense of its place and time in the flow of human events.

Wupatki National Monument, for example, near Sunset Crater, Arizona, is compelling in its desolation. Desert winds blow around the well-laid, well-preserved stone masonry walls of compact, apartment-like buildings. The adjacent slopes of Sunset Crater are still and barren. Only the black volcanic sand and fine pebbles shift ever so slightly in the ceaseless wind. Wupatki seems like the ancient counterpart to a western ghost town as portrayed in a modern movie—wind and dust, bare walls, empty buildings haunted by the echoes of voices long gone. Once a vibrant farming district with soils enriched by volcanic nutrients, the scene is now desolate and forlorn.

Mesa Verde National Park, a natural and cultural wonder in southwestern Colorado, displays an entirely different character. Verdant hills, snowcapped mountains, and high, wooded mesas form a natural picture frame for Mesa Verde's almost perfect cliff houses. Mug House, Sprucetree House, and Cliff Palace, like all the other major ruins in the park, are neat, compact, well built, and geometrical. Set against soaring cliff faces, they are nearly everyone's idea of the grandest villages in the ancient Southwest. But much about Mesa Verde remains a riddle. Who were the builders? What languages did they speak? What names did they call themselves? Where and who are their descendants? Some archaeologists have hazarded partial answers, but we still do not know for certain. As grand as it is, Mesa Verde remains a half-written chapter in an old history book.

Gila Cliff Dwellings National Monument. Photograph by O. C. Hinman.
Courtesy Museum of New Mexico, negative number 6205.

An ancient village whose character is even more enigmatic than Mesa Verde's is Gila Cliff Dwellings National Monument, in southwestern New Mexico. Like Mesa Verde, it rests in high country. In 1200 CE, this pueblo, tucked into a shady alcove in a sheer cliff face, was the only "cliff palace" in southern New Mexico. By Mesa Verde standards, it was a modest one. Judging from the pottery found in the ruins, researchers believe some ancestral Pueblo people from west-central New Mexico moved south after Chacoan society declined in the 1100s and took up a precarious existence amid remnants of a related society that archaeologists call Mogollon. The Gila community abandoned its cliff dwelling in the late 1200s, just as the Mesa Verdeans did theirs. No one knows where they went or why they had traveled so far south in the first place.

A place with a powerful character even today—and special significance for ancient events on the Pajarito Plateau—is Chaco Canyon, New Mexico. There, clusters of massive sandstone "great houses," built several centuries before those at Mesa Verde, stand preserved in Chaco Culture National Historical Park, also a UNESCO World Heritage Site. At Chaco,

Aerial view of Pueblo Bonito, in Chaco Canyon, New Mexico. The oldest and smallest rooms, built in the late 800s CE, are in the center-rear of the edifice, along the semicircular wall. Newer rooms line the plaza's front wall (foreground), built just a few decades before Chacoan regional society collapsed in the 1130s. Large kivas encircle the immense plaza. © Baker Aerial Archaeology—Tom Baker.

the timeless, desert-blue sky hangs above rock and sage, bright yellow-orange globe mallows, rabbit brush, stunted junipers, red-brown earth, and red-brown buildings. Pueblo Bonito, with its 332 ground-floor rooms, circular kivas, and banded masonry walls, is Chaco's crown jewel. In the classic Chaco style, row upon row of sandstone slabs were laboriously hand chinked with millions of stone chips. Both the quality and the cost of such construction, unequaled anywhere north of Mexico, are still astonishing a thousand years later. Ironically, this iconic banded stonework, which now graces casinos, courthouses, and high-end homes throughout New Mexico, was invisible under the layers of off-white plaster that graced Chaco's great houses in their heyday.

Chaco Canyon's "persona" is awesome, radiating a sense of power. In their day, the inhabitants of Pueblo Bonito surely believed fervently in the potency of their place on the landscape. Even the great broken crag of Threatening Rock, forming part of the cliff just behind Pueblo Bonito and carefully braced up in ancient times, did not dare to fall and crush the

Cliff Palace, at Mesa Verde, Colorado. The simpler masonry at this post-Chaco village, with its larger blocks, required much less labor than the banded Chacoan walls. Note the towers, where grain was stored. Photograph by Jesse L. Nusbaum, 1907. Courtesy Museum of New Mexico, negative number 60649.

rear of the pueblo until the afternoon of January 21, 1941—eight hundred years after the town's abandonment. Pueblo Bonito and the other great houses in Chaco Canyon symbolize ancient North America's greatest political and economic power. They also made up the costliest Southwestern society until modern Anglo-America swallowed New Mexico. Not surprisingly, Pueblo Indian peoples today all claim to be connected to, or descended from, those who built Pueblo Bonito.

Chaco Canyon arouses strong emotions in the traveler, but one is never more than a visitor there. To outsiders it offers no sense of belonging. Chaco Canyon belongs—has always belonged—to the souls of those who built in it, lived in it, and died in it. The raw power of Chaco Canyon is seductive to a modern American society obsessed with power, but, New Age hopes aside, it does not share its power with casual visitors of any kind.

Bandelier National Monument is very different in character from these other Southwestern places. Perhaps it is simply the Pajarito Plateau's crystalline air, at more than sixty-five hundred feet above sea level. Perhaps it is the remarkable views across the monument's craggy, volcanic tuff mesas, or the forested simplicity of Juniper Campground, or the solitude of the trail to the Shrine of the Stone Lions that makes Bandelier seem friendlier and more peaceful. It could even be the striking contrast between Frijoles Canyon's homey sense of community and old-fashioned efficiency—so important to the survival of Pueblo society—and Chaco's more "American"-style penchant for power and excess that so softens Bandelier's aspect. Most likely, the monument's special emotional appeal derives from its known human story—a saga that connects the ancestral Pueblo past to the vibrant world of contemporary Pueblo descendants.

Frijoles Canyon, the centerpiece of Bandelier National Monument, is a remarkably restful place. From the tree-shaded valley floor, the traveler, standing by a sparkling creek, looks up into a magical world where great tuff cliffs frame shadowed cave rooms and where immense rock promontories jut toward the heavens. Even the sky on the Pajarito Plateau seems a purer shade of turquoise than at any other place on earth. That the people of modern Cochiti Pueblo, a Keres-speaking community of several thousand residents just a few miles south of Tyuonyi, are descended from the dwellers of the monument's canyons brings a message of hope to an industrial America

Cochiti Pueblo. Photograph by John K. Hillers, 1880. Courtesy Museum of New Mexico, negative number 2493.

that offers little calm and an increasingly fragile sense of sustainability. By realistically and pragmatically facing some daunting changes in climate and ecology, these people prevailed.

The seasons, too, are special at Bandelier. Each night in late summer, a chill breeze rises gently up the canyon, smelling of autumn even before autumn arrives. In late winter, at Painted Cave, the midday sun infuses ancient rock with the delicate warmth of a coming spring. On a bright springtime morning atop the higher mesas, warmed air, rising from black basalt cliffs near the Rio Grande, nudges a gentle breeze over the lip of the mesas. The breeze carries the sharp scent of pine needles in anticipation of summer. This is a subtle place, alive with changing shadows, unexpected colors, and its own private seasons. Sunlight yesterday, rain today, snow tomorrow.

From behind the visitor center at Bandelier Monument, facing west, one looks up the canyon toward the village of Tyuonyi. The oldest villages lie above on the mesa tops—a Bandelier of even more ancient yesterdays. The visitor center, built during the Great Depression, is full of life and color. Its shaded courtyards and verandas accommodate crowds of visitors year-round. Hummingbirds flicker through its flagstoned courtyards. It is the Bandelier of today. And as one hikes down Frijoles Canyon, each ruin is more recent than the last, until one arrives in the contemporary Rio Grande Indian pueblos. Their unborn generations will no doubt venerate the ancient shrines above Frijoles Canyon just as their parents do now— this is the Bandelier of tomorrow.

The monument's name carries a special story, too. More than a century ago, a man named Adolph Bandelier, accompanied by Cochiti Indian guides, traversed a rugged, long-abandoned trail to look down into Frijoles Canyon. It was October 1880, and Bandelier was no longer young—like the canyon, he had already experienced many of his yesterdays. Born in Switzerland in the summer of 1840, he had come to the United States as a boy of eight. He spent his youth as a farm boy in a small German-Swiss community near St. Louis, Missouri. Later, he spent the first part of his adulthood in St. Louis, miscast, bored, and unfulfilled, working in a bank.

By his early thirties, the multilingual Bandelier was deeply immersed in a passionate personal diversion, that of researching New World Indian societies. A chance meeting with Lewis Henry Morgan, one of the nineteenth-century founders of anthropology, encouraged him further. By the 1870s he had published several library-based monographs and had attempted— rather unsuccessfully—a field study at the Rio Grande pueblo of Santo Domingo (now called Kewa Pueblo). When he first came to Frijoles Canyon at the age of forty, Bandelier had left behind the security of family, business, and a conventional Midwestern way of life. These days a psychologist might call his behavior a "mid-life crisis." Whatever Bandelier's motives, or the surprises to his immediate family, it was fortunate for posterity that a true romantic stepped to the rim of the canyon on that October day, looked down at the ruins now called Tyuonyi and at the cliff-face cave rooms, and pronounced them "the grandest thing I ever saw." In that instant Bandelier, the talented, self-styled anthropologist, was captivated by the area's special magic. Within several years he had moved from "self-styled" to "pioneer."

Adolph Bandelier did much for the emerging field of anthropology, not primarily as an original archaeological researcher but as a meticulous observer who brought both passion and perceptive vision to his work. He devoted most of the rest of his life to studying ancient societies, always in a spirit of romance. He spent twelve years, from 1880 to 1892, in the Southwest, with occasional interruptions for sojourns in Europe and Mexico. Remarkably, those dates fell precisely two hundred years after the great Pueblo Revolt of 1680–1692, in which Pueblo Indians drove every Spaniard out of the Rio Grande Valley and southward into what is now Mexico. During those twelve years, New Mexico's Pueblo Indian peoples tried one last time to fully reestablish the "old ways" that had existed before Spanish colonization in 1598. Diseases, droughts, and adaptations they had made to some Spanish agricultural practices confounded their efforts, and the Spaniards returned, without much resistance, in 1692. Two centuries later, Bandelier arrived as if on a schedule designed to commemorate the Pueblo society he was destined to immortalize. Were it not for Adolph Bandelier, the ancestral cradle of Cochiti and other pueblos would likely not be a national monument, named for him and meant to be preserved forever.

Few modern-day anthropologists would approve of Bandelier's subjective take on archaeological research methods. In the late nineteenth century, archaeology was still in its infancy. Techniques of excavation were just becoming organized and systematic, as were the identification and classification of differing pottery styles. Most of these developments were taking place in Europe and the Middle East, at famous sites such as Troy, Ur of the Chaldees, and the Great Pyramids in Egypt. Bandelier, the former banker, working in the still-isolated American Southwest, was not at the forefront of scientific methodology.

Instead, Bandelier's unique contributions to the monument that bears his name were respect and fascination for Indian society—a fascination that was nearly obsessive. He so deeply immersed himself in the culture of Cochiti Pueblo that he helped pioneer the anthropologist's now standard technique of "participant observation." His intense inquisitiveness, coupled with a prodigious ability to read quickly, assimilate information, and fastidiously record everything he heard and saw, gave us his spectacular *Journals*. These volumes, carefully edited and annotated by Charles Lange and Carroll Riley and published by the University of New Mexico Press in 1966, are still essential references for Pueblo Indian society and the many ruins Bandelier visited more than a century ago.

In the end, Bandelier left us more than his scholarly journals. Throughout the 1880s he wrote newspaper dispatches from places such as "Frijoles

Canyon," "The Pajarito, New Mexico Territory," and "Near Santa Fe, in New Mexico Territory." The earliest articles were published in St. Louis, and later his pieces appeared in some prominent East Coast, big-city newspapers, bringing him a few dollars of badly needed income.

By 1890 Bandelier was broke, estranged from part of his St. Louis family, and in need of money to sustain a European trip, so he wrote a novel portraying ancient life in Frijoles Canyon as he had reconstructed it from his studies. His book, *The Delight Makers*, not quite fact and not quite fiction, may well be one of the first books written in the increasingly popular style sometimes called creative nonfiction, or "faction." *The Delight Makers* was a literary success in its time and is still available in almost any bookstore specializing in the Southwest. Precious few books remain in print for more than a century, so *The Delight Makers* has become a true classic.

The very title of Bandelier's novel captures one special characteristic of Bandelier National Monument. Bandelier understood, a century ago, that Frijoles Canyon and the Pajarito Plateau were not like the Chaco country. Chaco Canyon sits uneasy beneath a restless sky, in a whirlwind of dust, chaotic and tragic. It is a place not at peace with itself, even nine centuries after its Puebloan inhabitants left. It is a place where, some say, the wailing of ancient mothers can still be heard at night echoing from the starlit walls of Pueblo Bonito. In contrast, Frijoles Canyon is full of quiet sunlight, curious animals, little birds, and peaceful innocence. It is a place where "delight makers" might truly have walked the earth. It is also a place where real treaties were once made between Keres speakers of the southern Pajarito Plateau and Tewa speakers of the northern district.

During Bandelier's years in New Mexico, perhaps in response to having escaped an earlier life he perceived as misspent, he seems to have experienced a heightening of his senses. He saw, smelled, tasted, touched, heard, and dreamed with unusual clarity, recording most of it for posterity. Then, as now, New Mexico was a remarkable place, full of sights, sounds, and people exotic to a Midwesterner.

Adolph Bandelier died in comparative poverty while in Seville, Spain, just as World War I began in 1914. He was at last doing research in the magnificent Archives of the Indies, his dream of many years. Nearly three-quarters of a century after his death, and after much bureaucratic wrangling, his ashes were scattered over the monument that now carries his name.

Visitors to Bandelier National Monument have a special opportunity to understand, appreciate, and respect the human saga that took place there. They are free to smell, to look, to listen, and to savor all the delights that the monument holds. And those delights are many, including the Cochiti drum makers who come each summer to show visitors how cottonwood and deer hide can be made to speak in ancient rhythms.

Unlike many other national parks, Bandelier Monument was not created just because of its natural beauty and its unusual flow of seasons. It was created to celebrate, protect, and preserve the heritage and cultural treasures of the people who once lived in it—people whose descendants still live nearby. Unlike Wupatki, Mesa Verde, Chaco Canyon, Gila Cliff Dwellings, and most of the other archaeological parks and monuments in the Southwest, Bandelier is not a dusty book already closed on the past. It is a window through which one can look back into yesterday or enjoy today or dream about a thousand summers from now. Archaeologists, like other monument visitors, are struck by this sensation of past and future. From Tyuonyi's circular room blocks, they, too, look to the high western mesas, with their even older sites, many of them uncharted until the 1980s and 1990s. To the east they look down the canyon to the Rio Grande, along which lie the living, breathing, subtly changing, modern-day Rio Grande pueblos.

As I was writing *The Magic of Bandelier*, this volume's predecessor, the first major archaeological survey of Bandelier National Monument was just being launched. For the first time, government archaeologists were walking large parts of the monument, finding and recording all its different kinds of archaeological remains, large and small. Only a few years earlier, National Park Service archaeologist Robert Powers had estimated that roughly five hundred archaeological sites existed in the approximately fifty square miles of the monument. By the time I finished my book manuscript in 1989, the number stood at eight hundred, and I surmised that as many as three thousand sites might eventually be found, spanning the centuries from 10,000 BCE ("before the common era") to 1600 CE.

The Bandelier survey, which Robert Powers directed from 1985 to 1991, was a major accomplishment. It increased the number of recorded archaeological sites to about nineteen hundred, generated at least eleven technical reports and papers, and eventually led to the interpretive book *The Peopling of Bandelier*, edited by Powers. Most important, survey work continues in Bandelier today, under the direction of monument archaeologist Rory Gauthier.

By July 2009, according to Gauthier, almost another thousand sites had been located since the Powers survey, bringing the total number recorded inside the monument boundaries to 2,896. Hundreds of these recently discovered sites have been identified as dating to the Archaic period, or between roughly 5000 BCE and 300 or 400 CE, adding much to our knowledge of a previously little-known era at Bandelier. Gauthier estimates that about 78 percent of the monument has been surveyed, meter by meter. The remaining areas consist mostly of steep mesa walls and rugged mountain flanks. Bandelier's astonishing density of archaeological sites is unmatched anywhere else in the Southwest.

Bandelier Monument makes up only one-sixth of the entire Pajarito Plateau, which covers more than three hundred square miles. Deep canyons separated by high mesas dissect the plateau from east to west, and on nearly every mesa top lie ancient, tuff-block-masonry settlements. Every canyon below shelters even more archaeological sites. A complete survey of the plateau would, when combined with information from the monument alone, yield a database of probably ten thousand to fifteen thousand sites.

The people of the Pajarito came and went for thousands of years, and their discarded artifacts—pieces of pottery, bits of stone tools, occasionally an arrowhead or an abandoned grinding stone—can be found virtually anywhere in the monument. Examples can be seen in displays at the visitor center. It is against the law to move or take artifacts, and worse, it destroys the past. Some archaeological sites are marked by perhaps only a dozen pottery fragments, each the size of a thumbnail. Removing any of them can forever destroy the ability of a field archaeologist to assign a relative date to that site.

Modern archaeologists seldom carry away artifacts, either. They regularly determine the general age of a site by looking at a few dozen fragments of pottery on the ground surface. They mark the location of each fragment on a field survey form, pick it up, examine it under a magnifying hand lens, record its characteristics, and then put it back in its original place. They can tell from the kind of clay the vessel was made from, the kinds of fine inclusions, or "temper," in the clay, such as sand or ground rock, and the style of decorations on its surface approximately when the pot was made. The loss of just one or a few shards might eliminate the vital piece of evidence revealing when people once lived, worked, or camped at that spot on the landscape.

With the protection of the National Park Service and of knowledgeable visitors, the potential for further discovery in Bandelier is remarkable and exciting. Some of that discovery will come through continued survey. The rest will have to come from excavation. Many researchers doubt that the final story of archaeology at Bandelier will have been written even a century from now. Some archaeologists once maintained that no Archaic period sites, or at least very few, existed in the monument. By now, several hundred have been found, and some have been excavated at the lower elevations now under Cochiti Reservoir.

In the high country of the Jemez Mountains, within twenty miles of Bandelier Monument, where thickets of Gambel's oak form along the creeks and on protective ridges, one finds many small, smooth, brown stream cobbles that were once used like pestles to mash acorns against larger, flat mortar stones, in the Southwest called *metates*. The hand stones, called one-hand manos (*mano* means "hand" in Spanish), often litter the landscape near dense stands of smallish oaks. Similar finds have now been made in the monument itself. One-hand manos were among the more common kinds of artifacts found by Powers's survey team, by the Archaic period specialist Bradley Vierra in the 1990s, and during Gauthier's subsequent work. They are critical clues needed to fill in a sketchy chapter about the Archaic period in Bandelier's long story, and I have more to say about them later.

Whether one visits Bandelier to discover something about the past or merely to seek peace, it is a place of ceaseless beauty. Its high mesas look east toward the Sangre de Cristo Mountains. Below them lies the small city of Santa Fe and yet another chapter in New Mexico's history. From the unique vistas of Bandelier Monument, one can look to the past, gaze down to today's busy world, or imagine another six hundred generations of life to come. That is the special public persona of Bandelier.

To an evolution-focused anthropologist, the monument's special persona derives from its role in the transformation of ancestral Pueblo society after the fall and decline of the spectacular Chacoan culture of the 900s to 1100s CE. That fall required the survivors to make urgent adaptations to the harsh realities imposed by a fragmented and chaotic social order, a scarcity of resources, and an economic and ecological disaster of epic proportions. What is now Bandelier National Monument was not just one crucible of that transformation; it was the heart of the most important one. And a new kind of efficiency was the primary fluxing agent in that crucible's transforming melt.

Efficiency mattered, above all else, to the survival of Chaco's descendants. In contemporary America, it still matters. In times of scarcity, the efficient prevail.

PART TWO

The Archaeology

of

Bandelier

and the

Pajarito Plateau

A cave kiva in Frijoles Canyon. Courtesy National Park Service,
Bandelier National Monument.

B andelier National Monument tilts eastward toward the rising sun. Its fifty square miles of rugged canyons and mesas sweep upward from the Rio Grande on the east, at an elevation of about 5,300 feet above sea level, to the summit of Cerro Grande on the north, at 10,199 feet.

Natural historians think of Bandelier as a particular place on the east face of the Jemez Mountains atop a sloping bench known as the Pajarito ("little bird") Plateau. Much of this tilted, rocky table is formed of deep layers of volcanic tuff, or hardened ash, that exploded from the Jemez volcano—now a collapsed crater known as the Valles Caldera—more than a million years ago.

Archaeologists, on the other hand, think of Bandelier Monument as an island of archaeological treasures in the vast landscape of the greater Southwest, where more than several hundred thousand sites are known. The monument was established in 1916, primarily to celebrate and promote Tyuonyi, the spectacular circular village in Frijoles Canyon. Most of the nearby cliff houses were built sometime between the early 1200s and the 1400s CE, so older guidebooks often give the impression that Bandelier figured in only several centuries of ancient Southwestern life. But artifacts found in the monument now include examples from every major cultural horizon in New Mexico: the Paleo-Indian (about 9500 to 5500 BCE); the Archaic (about 5000 BCE to 1 CE); the Basketmaker (about 300 to 800 CE); and the Pueblo (about 800 to 1600 CE). True, the monument's visitor center celebrates the canyon's heyday, between 1300 and 1550, but the human drama began to unfold there more than ten thousand years ago.

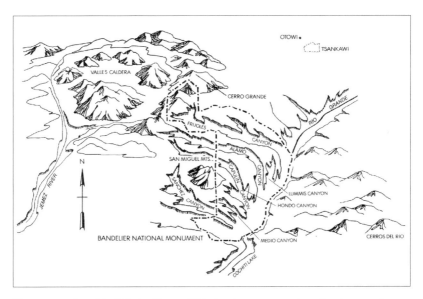

The topography of the Pajarito Plateau. This drawing corresponds to the photograph shown on page 23. Courtesy Bandelier National Monument, National Park Service.

Ancient Hunter-Gatherer Society

The Paleo-Indian Period

S ome archaeologists believe the ancestors of Bandelier's first tool makers worked their way across the "dry" (in fact marshy in many spots) Bering land bridge, which for a time connected what we now call Siberia with Alaska. During the last great ice age (the Pleistocene geological epoch), when huge amounts of sea water froze into glacial ice packs, sea levels dropped. A majority of researchers currently believes North America was first populated as early as thirteen thousand years ago by small, successive migrations of nomadic hunters following animal herds. Others argue for an earlier entry by people who fished and pursued ocean mammals from skin boats, their primary means of travel. I think both scenarios are likely.

Whatever their means of arrival, these long-vanished people left many poorly dated traces of their campsites on this continent. A few campsites, however, are well dated and give us a rough working outline of events. We know that these early arrivals already possessed fire, brought dogs, and made a variety of stone and bone tools before reaching Alaska on foot or the Northwest Coast by boat. Their descendants soon developed finely flaked lance heads of remarkable quality. Because archaeologists know nothing of their language, their names for themselves, or many of the nonmaterial details of their daily lives, they call these people collectively "Paleo-Indians" (old Indians) wherever their stone tools are found.

No one knows precisely when Paleo-Indians first came to what is now the U.S. Southwest, but the earliest well-dated campsites of such people appeared between 9000 and 10,000 BCE. By roughly 9500 BCE (the dates shift subtly as academic debates rage), the first groups of these hunters known to archaeologists were living in present-day New Mexico. Their camps, called "Clovis" sites, are named for a distinctive style of stone lance head first found near Clovis, New Mexico, about two hundred miles east-southeast of the Pajarito Plateau.

Archaeologists have found a few Clovis lance heads, nine thousand to ten thousand years old, in Bandelier National Monument. Several of these were fashioned from Pedernal chert, a type of stone obtained from

The Pajarito Plateau (left) is sheltered by the Jemez Mountains to the west and etched by east-trending canyons that empty into the Rio Grande. © Baker Aerial Archaeology— Tom Baker.

an ancient quarry just thirty miles away, at the foot of Pedernal Peak. Others appear to be made of cherts from the high plains of Texas. Obviously, Clovis hunters ranged widely. Just how many Clovis tool makers lived in or around the monument is unclear, because archaeologists have tended to focus on the larger, Puebloan ruins and pay little attention to scattered early finds.

Following the discovery of North America's first Paleo-Indian sites in the early 1900s, most archaeologists became convinced that Clovis hunters were primarily plains dwellers. This was because the larger Clovis sites then known lay consistently on the rolling plains of New Mexico, west Texas, and Colorado. Most such sites held traces of group hunting or scavenging for mammoths and other now-extinct species common to the late glacial period. By the 1950s and 1960s, Clovis-style sites were being found in many other parts of the United States and in Canada and Mexico. Ongoing research is beginning to fill in details about how these earliest hunter-foragers used the whole environment available to them, as it existed nearly ten thousand years ago.

As the last ice age slipped away nine thousand to ten thousand years ago, summers were an estimated ten or eleven degrees cooler, on average, than they are nowadays. Tall stands of ponderosa pines grew five hundred to a thousand feet lower in elevation than they do today, so Frijoles Canyon and the mesas above it would have been more densely wooded in early Paleo-Indian times. Summers were particularly cool and wet, and the seasons were not nearly as well defined as they are now. Long-extinct giant animals ("megafauna") still roamed New Mexico; mastodons, dire wolves, giant ground sloths, camels, and horses all coexisted with the early nomads. Probably few people traveled or camped at any one time either in the monument itself or in the lowlands below Bandelier. In the Paleo-Indian world, life was an endless trek from campsite to campsite as small family bands followed game and gathered favorite berries and roots along the way. All the while, Clovis craftsmen made their beautiful tools, exercising particularly remarkable control over the thickness and width of the lance-head base. This was important for hafting the lance head securely to a socketed wood or bone foreshaft.

New Mexico's Clovis hunters were choosy about the stone from which they made their lance heads. Favored quarries have been identified at several places in Texas; at Sapello, north of Las Vegas, New Mexico; and at Pedernal Peak. Clovis tool makers also used obsidian—volcanic glass—from the Jemez Mountains and from Narbona (formerly Washington) Pass, high in the Chuska Mountains, more than a hundred miles to the west of Bandelier. Lance heads from those sources are often found hundreds of miles from the quarries themselves. When stone from favorite sources was unavailable, hunters used local stone, primarily to make expedient, "throwaway" tools. Lance heads of both local and imported stone have been found in Bandelier, so archaeologists infer one of two scenarios: either permanent local populations of Clovis hunters frequented the area and traded with others for distant stone, or eastern plainsmen stayed long enough on high-country hunts to exhaust their supplies of treasured Texas cherts. Either way, the occasional use of local stone, coupled with scattered

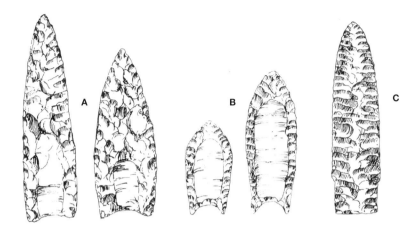

Paleo-Indian lance heads. A, Clovis; B, Folsom; C, Scottsbluff. Folsom points, dating to about 9000 BCE, were the first tools found imbedded in the bones of extinct bison—conclusive proof that humans inhabited North America long before the common era. Reproduced from *Prehistory of the Southwest*, by Linda Cordell. Courtesy Academic Press, Inc.

finds of (usually broken) lance points at elevations of sixty-five hundred to eight thousand feet, indicates that the Bandelier area was important to early hunters in still unresearched ways.

Later Paleo-Indian lance heads have been found elsewhere on the Pajarito Plateau, among them the types that archaeologists have labeled Folsom (7000 to 8000 BCE) and Scottsbluff (about 6500 BCE). Folsom lance heads, like Clovis ones, were "fluted," or grooved like a bayonet blade, but they show even finer workmanship. Those found near the monument were made of white chalcedony, a stone available from the ancient Pedernal quarry, a day's walk to the northwest. The later Scottsbluff points were long blades, carefully flaked but without a flute. Perhaps they were used for skinning large game.

Both Folsom and later Scottsbluff hunters favored as their large game the somewhat smaller species of bison that had evolved by this time. By the end of the Folsom period, the mastodons, dire wolves, sabertooths, and other giant fauna of the last ice age were gone, victims of a post-glacial change in climate to warmer and dryer conditions. By the time so-called Eden hunting bands roamed the northern Rio Grande Valley, around 6000 BCE, the climate, vegetation, and animal life were much more similar to those of modern times. By then the tall ponderosas grew only on the high mesas, and piñons and junipers flourished on lower ones, just as they do today.

In New Mexico, most known sites of the early Paleo-Indian periods have been found in open grasslands, which are lower in elevation than Bandelier Monument. There, bison lived in huge, migratory herds. In some seasons or in poor years, however, perhaps no bison at all roamed the lowlands east of the Pajarito. At those times, upland species such as deer, elk, and bighorn sheep might have been the most important sources of meat, hides, and bones. Then, as now, the deep canyons of the present-day monument—Frijoles, Alamo, and Capulin Canyons—would have provided game, fine campsites, piñon nuts, firewood, and water. Seasonal hunting and foraging, coupled with occasional forays to collect stone from Pedernal Peak or the less frequently used obsidian from the Jemez Mountains, most likely explain the Paleo-Indian artifacts now found thinly scattered on the Pajarito Plateau.

Only isolated lance heads from the Paleo-Indian era have been found in Bandelier Monument itself. This is unsurprising, because these ancient people required vast territories for foraging. But two Paleo-Indian hearths have been discovered on a mesa top near the Rio Grande north of the monument. They tell us that people once camped there, but absent other artifacts, it is impossible to know whether these were the cooking fires of one or more families or of a few hunters watching game below. Millennia later, Apache hunter-gatherer bands also camped in the lower canyons, on nearby riverbanks, and on mesa escarpments overlooking rich game land between the Pajarito and the Rio Grande Valley. Among these seventeenth- to nineteenth-century hunters, it was common to gather for buffalo hunts in the late spring or mid-fall. After a successful hunt, the large parties scattered, and small family groups sought sheltered canyons in which to prepare winter camps, such as those found in the Gallinas River canyon near contemporary Las Vegas, New Mexico. The Bandelier area offers such campsites, too, but it would not have supported more than a few families at a time during the Paleo-Indian period.

Plausible estimates of population densities for the Paleo-Indian subperiods are always written in terms of how many square miles (640 acres) were required to support one adult using ancient hunter-gatherer technology—not in terms of how many people could have been supported in just one square mile, as we think of population density today. The packing of many people into permanent villages, towns, and cities is nearly always a function of the labor-and-energy-hungry world that followed the adoption of agriculture. The Paleo-Indian people of Bandelier lived in a world in which nearly all energy was provided daily by the food they ate, stored in their bodies, and expended the next day while foraging and hunting. If some calories went temporarily unburned, the ordinary result was an increase in body fat, not an increase in archaeologically detectable artifacts. From studies of living hunter-gatherers, researchers estimate that Paleo-Indian people "worked" only about five hundred hours a year in activities required to make a living. That figure stands in stark contrast to the two thousand or more hours of work a year imposed on most of us since the seventeenth century.

At around 10,000 to 8000 BCE, Bandelier's fifty square miles likely supported no more than several small, family, traveling bands at a time. That fact alone may explain why no large Paleo-Indian camps have yet been found there. The Paleo-Indian era was a time when the world was vast, people were few, and daily life was excruciatingly slow to change. In short, it was a time ruled by modesty of consumption and, above all, energy efficiency on a scale now almost unimaginable. That efficiency sustained one version or another of the Paleo-Indian way of life for more than five thousand years. It was an almost indefinitely sustainable cultural adaptation. Over the millennia, this would not be the last time efficient behavior became the key to a society's sustainability in Bandelier Monument and its vicinity.

From Hunters to Gatherers

The Archaic Period

The era of Paleo-Indian hunters ended as climate in the American South-west changed fully to modern conditions. Neither the climatic nor the cultural transition was smooth. Between roughly 5000 and 3500 BCE, the climate rapidly became much hotter and drier, during a period clima-tologists call the Altithermal. Bison had already been evolving into suc-cessively smaller subspecies as the Southwest grew more arid. But the Altithermal was not subtle, and local bison now became scarce or may have disappeared altogether as remnant herds sought refuge to the north, in the cooler grasslands of present-day Colorado, Wyoming, the Dakotas, and southern Canada.

According to an archaeological interpretation in vogue about fifty years ago, by roughly 5500 to 5000 BCE a large region around Bandelier National Monument supported no humans at all. Some archaeologists remain con-vinced that the harsh, dry Altithermal created such a situation. Others argue convincingly that remnant populations hung on, adapted, modified their tool kits, and managed actually to grow in numbers, possibly augmented by later immigrations of people from what is now Arizona or the interior desert of California. Whatever the case, a new style of living arose in New Mexico beginning around 5000 BCE. Characterized by far more intensive use of wild plants and much less wandering, this period is called simply the Archaic, or the Desert Archaic. Intensive plant collecting meant that peo-ple expended more labor in gathering and processing foods that provided fewer calories by volume than meat did. In terms of labor investment, this adaptation was less efficient than hunting, but it cut an entire link out of the food chain. The net mathematics of this adjustment are striking, as outlined in the accompanying box.

More work to produce low-caloric-density plant foods seems not, at first glance, to be a winning strategy. But this shift had consequences that changed the course of subsequent Southwestern history. First, it led to the necessity and habit of intensive seed collection, which, three thousand years later, factored heavily into the adoption of early agriculture. Second, it made

Per Capita Caloric Costs of Large Game Hunting and Foraging versus Intensive Seed Collecting and Small Game Hunting

If the average Paleo-Indian adult, weighing 135 pounds, invested 500 hours a year in the medium-intensity work of foraging and hunting game, his or her basal (at rest) metabolism—1,500 calories per day, or 547,500 calories per year—would have been his or her largest caloric and energetic cost by far. At 250 calories an hour, the 500 hours of medium-intensity work would have added another 125,000 calories annually, for a basic per capita expenditure of 672,500 calories a year.

Body size declines somewhat as protein intake decreases, which would have happened if Archaic people trimmed their hunting by half and tripled their foraging for plants. With an average body weight of 125 pounds—not a dramatic weight or size loss during a climate crisis such as the Altithermal—basal metabolism would have declined to roughly 503,000 calories per year. Labor costs, however, would have risen. On one hand, cutting traditional hunting by half, to 250 hours a year, would have reduced its cost to 37,500 calories. But on the other, increasing the time spent in intensive plant gathering to 750 hours a year, at a slightly greater work intensity—say, 275 calories per hour—would have raised the cost of foraging to 206,250 calories per year. Together with basal metabolism, these energy expenditures bring the maintenance total to a minimum of 746,750 calories per person per year.

far more raw calories available, for the following reason. When people eat herbivorous game animals, they convert the animals' muscle and fat into their own body structure. But approximately 90 percent of the calories in the plants that the animals ate to reach their huntable weight have been lost to waste and inefficient metabolism. To put it in modern terms, an average ear of corn contains 70 calories, but corn-fed cows fix only 10 percent of those calories, or 7 calories per ear equivalent, into their body mass. Correspondingly, when you eat beef, you fix only seven-tenths of one feed corn-ear equivalent calorie in your body. The energetic return from feedlot, corn-stuffed cattle is disastrously wasteful of food that humans could otherwise consume with little processing. In a massive food shortage, vegetarians win, if they cut out the ungulate "middle man" and eat the ungulates' own food. In nature, this is why meat-eating predators are few, relative to their prey. They are too metabolically expensive to be numerous.

The Altithermal forced Archaic people to trim back their role as predators and partially fill the food niche of the ungulates—deer, elk, and bison—that had become so scarce as the climate grew drier. In short, it forced a brilliant ecological restructuring of humans' overall niche in their ecosystem—a far more efficient and abundant niche, if they were willing to do more work.

The third change created by the shift to eating more plant foods was a strong impetus to find ways to get more calories from those foods. Archaic people developed complex methods for processing the roots of agaves, which grow at high elevations, and of yuccas, which prefer the lowlands, as well as acorns and other starchy plants. The new methods produced high-carbohydrate meals—and a windfall for archaeologists, in the form of roasting pits in which plants were cooked with heated stones. Often visible on the ground as piles of reddish, fire-cracked, burnt rocks, the remains of these pits are a hallmark of campsites of the so-called Jay period, the earliest of the Archaic subperiods in northern New Mexico. These campsites tend to be situated near the heads of canyons throughout the northern mountains. More such sites will no doubt be found and excavated in Bandelier and on the Pajarito as archaeological work continues.

Study of the Archaic is still in flux. One current trend is to downplay the whole idea of an Archaic period and instead to classify such sites according to distinct "tool traditions"—that is, to look at the characteristics of stone tools over time in one part of the Southwest rather than try to identify similarities among tools everywhere at a particular time. Another trend is to focus on patterns of human movement across the landscape—"mobility," for short—followed by hunter-foragers as opposed to collector-hunters. Such research is intriguing, but it skirts the essence of the Archaic period, which was a series of groundbreaking behavioral responses to a catastrophically changing climate, vegetation, and fauna.

The Altithermal brought a crisis of oscillating heat and drought that fairly quickly made the late Paleo-Indian way of life impossible. The great herds of bison diminished or died out. The geographic range and migratory behavior of surviving bison changed enough that the seemingly timeless ways of hunting, trekking, and relying on meat yielded ever less success. Following bison made little sense once the animals had moved several hundred miles north, out of a local New Mexico hunting band's territory, especially if the intervening landscape was territory already held by other bands.

During the harsh, dry Altithermal, then, a singular adaptation emerged. Hunting-gathering was, as a practical matter, inverted into a pattern of gathering and processing plant foods and "hunting when we can." The gathering was primarily of resources such as yucca roots (or agave roots on the Pajarito Plateau), grass seeds, berries, piñon nuts, and acorns. The urgent search for new resources was based in ancient behaviors but enriched by experimentation in processing plant foods newly emphasized in the diet. In the course of these emergency changes, early Archaic people set in motion a trend that is still pertinent to today's world economy. By obtaining a large percentage of their food from plants, they stopped acting like the keystone predator species at the top of the food chain and began acting ecologically more like the vegetarian deer, elk, and bison that their Paleo-Indian forebears had hunted for meat.

Because only about 10 percent of the calories an animal ingests from plants is fixed in edible meat or bone, Archaic people could obtain nine times more calories by eating protein-rich collected seeds and, for carbohydrates, carefully processed plant foods than they could by chasing down the diminishing sources of meat. Thus, the hallmark of the early Archaic was a strategic move nearly a full step down on the food chain as a means of survival. The disadvantage was that both collecting and processing plant foods required more hours of work and fuel energy per edible calorie than had hunting large game. The dynamics that linked all peoples of the early Archaic were that they gathered plant resources more intensively than their Paleo-Indian predecessors, carried what they collected to base camps for complex processing, put in more hours of work, experimented more with new foods, and moved somewhat less across the landscape. All these practices required a change from the Paleo-Indian tool kit, in which lance heads and dart points predominated, to one in which grinding tools became much more important.

These emergency trends set the stage for later, full-blown Archaic collecting societies. They led to further increases in workloads over the centuries, to ever more confined geographic mobility, to larger social groups (to provide the extra labor), and to a balance between tradition and regular doses of innovation. From such landmark evolutionary changes are born new ages of humankind, among them the agriculture age and the Industrial Revolution.

The Archaic period saw the most important evolutionary changes in the history of the American Southwest. It still confounds many archaeologists, because as groups localized, some of them, by middle to later Archaic times, went back to emphasizing big-game hunting, which entails much less work when game animals are abundant. Because some archaeologists tend to rely on descriptions of "normal" or "standard" behavior that eschew variations between small groups, such differences in economic behavior can be perplexing. The idea that behavior and technology are easily reversible is difficult for researchers to integrate, especially those raised on Darwin's and Mendel's genetic versions of evolution. The unilinear evolution of the nineteenth century—basically, ever onward and upward—is alive and well in many of the narrow assumptions made in contemporary archaeological interpretations of ancient economies and technologies.

Until 1931, there was no "conclusive" (that is, widely accepted) proof that Paleo-Indian people existed. Therefore, the first anthropologists to work at what became Bandelier National Monument, including Adolph Bandelier and Edgar Lee Hewett, an archaeologist based in Santa Fe, worked on the eastern academic establishment's actively enforced assumption that no humans had lived in the Americas much more than three thousand or four thousand years before the common era. Even then the Archaic period, which was believed to mark the earliest human presence in the Western Hemisphere and to have begun not long before the beginning of the common era, attracted little sustained scholarly interest. In those early days, investigators working on the Pajarito Plateau looked almost exclusively at the several centuries during which people inhabited the cave rooms, cliff houses, and larger, well-known villages in Frijoles Canyon. This emphasis has changed only partly in the intervening century.

Lance heads, dart points, and knives (which are often mistaken for arrowheads) from the various Archaic subperiods are found in Bandelier Monument. Unlike Paleo-Indian tools, they are not rare. The majority of the earliest Archaic points, known as the Jay and Bajada types and dating roughly from 5000 to 3000 BCE, were fashioned from what is usually described as fine-grained basalt—actually dacite—which outcrops on the monument's lower, eastern margins, near the Rio Grande. The stone used to make the more numerous late Archaic tools, those dating from about 2000 BCE to 300 CE, depended on location and the kind of tool being manufactured.

As a generalization, most late Archaic points, or hunting tools, on the Pajarito Plateau were flaked from the premium obsidian found on the monument's high, western side. Tools such as scrapers, gravers, and burins, which people used for tasks like processing hides and making wooden objects, were fashioned primarily from two kinds of stone. One was the black basalt-dacite

Aerial view of Alamo Canyon on the Pajarito Plateau. The entire Bandelier area is crosscut by similar deep canyons. Note the dramatic changes in vegetation and the relative isolation of the canyon floor. © Baker Aerial Archaeology—Tom Baker, 1989.

from the monument area; the other consisted of lighter-colored cherts and chalcedony from the northern edge of the monument and beyond its boundaries, as far as the cliff dwellings known as Puye, some twelve miles north of Tyuonyi and the present-day visitor center. People probably traded in obsidian for points but used locally available stone for more expedient tools that would be discarded when worn out. Although some trade in obsidian is evident for the later Archaic, such exchange had become a social and economic driving force by the time Tyuonyi was built in the 1200s.

Like Paleo-Indian finds, these clues into Archaic adaptations on the Pajarito Plateau have not yet been fully pursued, but modern research into Archaic period technology and economy has begun both to the west and the east of the monument. A summary published by Bradley Vierra in *The Peopling of Bandelier* is highly informative.

Looking south, down Alamo Canyon to White Rock Canyon and Cochiti Reservoir, it is possible to see La Bajada Mesa, which straddles Interstate 25 near Cochiti Pueblo. During the Archaic period, the so-called

Bajada point, a stemmed lance head dating to about 3000 BCE, was commonly made in the area. Most Bajada points were flaked from the black, fine-grained to glassy dacite that forms the lower mesas jutting up from the Rio Grande. These mesas were laid down during a massive volcanic eruption earlier than the one that formed the higher, soft tuff mesas like those found on either side of Frijoles Canyon.

La Bajada Mesa, the small plateau known as the Caja del Rio just two miles east of the monument, and areas now submerged under Cochiti Reservoir supported increasingly large populations of Archaic people once the frightful heat of the Altithermal abated, from about 3000 BCE to the common era. The Archaic period archaeology of the now submerged Cochiti Reservoir area is among the most meticulously studied in the region. In the late 1970s, the University of New Mexico's Office of Contract Archaeology published four massive volumes of survey and analytical findings from its Cochiti Reservoir project, edited by project directors Jan Biella and Richard Chapman.

The majority of identified Archaic sites in and around the monument date from the middle to late Archaic, roughly between 2000 BCE and 300 CE. Thirty miles to the west, however, along the Rio Puerco, archaeologist Cynthia Irwin-Williams identified the local development of Archaic cultures beginning about 5000 BCE and continuing unbroken until just after the start of the common era. The Rio Puerco area, like the middle Rio Grande district near Albuquerque, shows both identifiable regional variations in details of tool types and the commonality of a focus on plant collecting in the daily economy.

People undoubtedly used the Bandelier Monument area throughout the Archaic period, especially the lower canyons near the Rio Grande. As the population increased throughout the region after about 1000 BCE, families began making greater use of the higher, western elevations as well, for both hunting and foraging. It is likely that site patterns and artifacts in the high country contrasted increasingly over time with those in the lower land now under Cochiti Reservoir. Most researchers believe Archaic people used the monument's forested uplands mostly for hunting deer and elk and collecting obsidian. But that picture of Archaic life seems too simplistic in light of recent discoveries. It is here that the grinding stones I mentioned earlier become important.

One-hand manos, so characteristic of the middle and later Archaic, have now been found throughout the monument's elevation zones. Their counterparts, the flat, irregularly shaped basin metates, are often found

Stone artifacts of the middle and late Archaic period from the Bandelier area. Items 1–7 are small, very hard hammerstones unique to the Pajarito Plateau. Items 8–10 are one-hand manos. Courtesy Los Alamos National Laboratory.

nearby. In the higher elevations, these stones were probably used to grind acorns in places where forest fires had cleared the conifers and allowed Gambel's oak to invade. Elsewhere, they were probably used to grind agave roots and wild grass seeds. Astonishingly, the metates still lie inverted on the ground, their shallow, abraded depressions facing earthward. According to Rory Gauthier, people left them that way to prevent water from pooling in them, only to freeze and then crack the valuable tool. In other words, the ancients who used these grinding stones more than a thousand years ago apparently once walked away intending to return. In doing so, they may inadvertently have protected detectable traces of the plant materials once ground on the stones. Minute particles might still be imbedded in the sandstone or vesicular basalt of some of the metates' grinding surfaces. Laboratory analysts can now identify such infinitesimal traces. Such research, if conducted, might go a long way toward fleshing out our understanding of food collecting patterns in different altitude zones.

For three thousand years or more, Archaic people on the Pajarito Plateau fashioned many of their dart points, knives, and scraping tools from obsidian found in the monument's high, western approaches to the Jemez caldera. Black or gray, sometimes banded obsidian came from a place now known as the Polvadera quarry, and glassy varieties came from an area called Obsidian Ridge. The use of Jemez Mountain obsidian became increasingly widespread throughout the Archaic period. By the early common era, tools of Jemez obsidian were being used over thousands of square miles in north-central New Mexico.

As in Paleo-Indian times, the monument's wooded mesas and sheltered canyons would have been important hunting territory for people who lived nearby. But Archaic people were, above all, plant collectors. Piñon nuts, acorns, and wild grass seeds were important storable, high-protein foods with which to augment game taken in the cold winters of northern New Mexico. So were pigweed seeds, wild potatoes, goosefoot, and a variety of wild berries available in the ponderosa pine forests. At somewhat lower elevations, the piñon-juniper zone offered, besides piñon nuts and acorns, wolfberries, a large variety of cacti, and many other seed-bearing plants.

West of the monument, across the Jemez Mountains, Rory Gauthier and I conducted an archaeological survey in the 1980s of previously unsurveyed, restricted land. We discovered large areas where Archaic people appeared to have intensively harvested acorns in the upper reaches of the piñon-juniper zone, along a prominent ridge about seven thousand feet in elevation. They ground the acorns into a protein-rich meal on the spot, leaving behind hundreds of one-hand manos. Remarkably, many of the manos were still in place in the circular depressions that people had ground out of the bedrock boulders fronting the ridge to serve as mortars. Such mortars, which

Obsidian, or volcanic glass. Ancestral Puebloans mined obsidian in the Jemez Mountains, where it formed during the eruption of the volcano that created the Valles Caldera. Courtesy National Park Service, Bandelier National Monument, 1964.

archaeologists call basin metates, were created by the twisting, grinding motions the Indian women made as they laboriously worked their one-hand manos—effective early "food processors." This site extends for nearly three quarters of a mile, and similar ones have now been found in Bandelier Monument.

By the end of Archaic times, in the early common era, local populations began to group themselves into small, scattered, semipermanent settlements. No such settlement has yet been found on monument land, but some wide, corner-notched lance heads, shaped rather like the ace of spades and characteristic of this time, have been discovered there. Archaeologists agree that the areas to the southwest of the Pajarito Plateau (near modern-day Jemez Pueblo), to the west (the Rio Puerco Valley), and to the east (the Rio Grande Valley) all supported modest populations of part-time horticulturalists between 500 BCE and 200–300 CE. In the lowlands surrounding Bandelier, shallow, circular pithouses (up to three feet deep) and food storage pits were being dug and used even before fired pottery was manufactured. The early storage pits are simple, circular holes in the ground, often two to three feet across and lined with rough sandstone slabs. They were an outgrowth of much earlier, smaller, and simpler pits that were adopted in late Paleo-Indian and very early Archaic times, when intensive seed collecting substantially replaced large game hunting at the peak of the Altithermal.

Few people realize that early "farmers" in New Mexico continued to depend heavily on hunting and foraging for more than a thousand years after corn was introduced from Mexico. The introduction of cultigens— corn, beans, and squash—did not radically alter Archaic lifestyles for many generations. The early corn, called *chapalote*, was very small cobbed and produced only modest harvests. Later, near the end of the pre-pottery era, about 300 BCE, a larger-cobbed corn with eight rows of kernels (*maiz de ocho*) was introduced into New Mexico along with other varieties, all probably from northwestern Mexico. This corn offered larger caloric yields, and small garden plots of it became increasingly important during the early common era.

The surveys conducted at Bandelier by Robert Powers, Janet Orcutt, and their colleagues in the late 1980s, and those that continue under Gauthier's supervision, have seriously modified earlier assumptions that Paleo-Indian and Archaic people seldom ventured into the higher woodlands of northern New Mexico. In the late 1970s and early 1980s, a team of archaeologists working for the Bureau of Indian Affairs on potential timber-sale land in places adjacent to the monument had found artifacts and small campsites from before the common era in virtually every timbered, mountainous area in which they systematically hunted for traces of these early foragers. The situation has proved to be no different in Bandelier.

The Evolutionary Consequences of Horticulture

The transition to small-scale horticulture in the greater Southwest was slow, complicated, and, in cultural evolutionary terms, utterly fascinating. Anthropologists' devotion to the topic of farming derives from the discipline's nineteenth-century founding perspectives. It was traditional to assume that "civilizations," too often vaguely defined as large, complex societies such as ancient Egypt, Greece, and Rome, all arose as a direct consequence of the adoption of agriculture. Earlier researchers generally ignored the smaller but still complex and highly structured societies that depended on abundant collected resources, such as fish from massive salmon runs, which gave rise to the United States' and Canada's Northwest Coast Haida and Tlingit cultures. And they long assumed that horticulture—the less intensive stage of agriculture, reliant on hand labor—quickly generated, rather like Thomas Edison's small, private laboratory, an agricultural enterprise analogous to the later commercial monoliths of General Electric and Western Electric.

As human products of the industrial age, early anthropologists believed the advantages of agriculture were so transparent and dramatic that they virtually ensured a rapid replacement of earlier technologies. A relatively brief but never formally defined period of innovative improvement gave way to an explosive rise of large, complex societies—just like the ones the anthropologists had grown up in.

But that simply did not happen in either the Southwest or, as it turns out, ancient Mexico. Instead, scattered families of intensive seed collectors —those most familiar with and dependent on wild plants rather than big game hunting—began slowly to invest somewhat more labor in planting, seasonally tending tiny plots of small-cobbed corn, beans, and squash during the middle Archaic period, from roughly 1800 to 1200 BCE. The practice of horticulture then spread, leading to small irrigation systems in the relatively densely populated vicinity of present-day Tucson, Arizona, before 1000 BCE and to modest, streamside cultivation in what is now southern New Mexico between about 500 BCE and 300 CE.

This trajectory is understandable if one factors in several realities important to researchers who style themselves "cultural energeticists." What makes a society large, powerful, and complex is not the genius of its culture so much as the raw energy that flows through it. That energy can be measured in calories. In order to get huge energy flows from the techniques of agriculture, one must first put more energy into the system to get it moving. For more than a millennium, the energy came from the direct hand labor of people who had to eat enough every day to process the calories needed for the next day's work. And horticulture, like raising plants in any other hand-tended garden, required a lot of work.

The need for more labor set off a cascade of enormous consequences that began to play out during the late Archaic period and during what archaeologists in northern New Mexico usually call the early Basketmaker period, a transitional time that archaeologist Cynthia Irwin-Williams named the En Medio period. First, it required people to eat more, so it intensified their food quest. Second, it induced greater demand for stored foodstuffs, to better equalize the calories available throughout the year. As a result, storage capacity expanded. The storage of food, rather like the storage of fuel in a car's gas tank, kept the momentum of change going during the food-poor seasons of the year, which once limited the growth of foraging-hunting societies throughout the world.

In the Southwest, people's need to store more food could be met only if they collected more wild seeds and nuts, enlarged their plots of corn, beans, and squash, or both. For a horticultural hamlet of the En Medio period, these economic realities meant that harvesting gardens and gathering seeds in the fall diverted labor away from the main annual hunt, which also took place in the fall. Simultaneously, investing more time and energy in cultivating crops and collecting seeds began to change people's reproductive decisions and family composition in unprecedented ways. A horticultural family requires more children, including daughters, to collect seeds (which is usually women's work in foraging societies) and to work in its small garden plots. The growth of family size resulting from the slow adoption of horticulture crucially altered the course of change that ended the Archaic period.

Old-style hunter-collectors are very sensitive to population density because they require vast, undisturbed territories in which to hunt and practice low-intensity collecting. They decidedly do not need more labor and larger families. If population density begins to rise in a region, they tend to engage in sexual and reproductive behaviors that restrict family size. Such behaviors typically include placing taboos on premarital sex, excluding young males from the marriage pool, and nursing children for long periods (nursing inhibits ovulation, so it helps keep women from getting pregnant again quickly). Women may induce abortions, and people occasionally practice infanticide, or the killing of newborns—mostly females, because sons presumably will become hunters and care for their parents in their old age. Highly successful hunters in such groups hold enormous prestige. Unsuccessful hunters and men who collect plants have neither prestige nor, at the extreme, wives.

By the beginning of the common era, when neighboring families of horticulturists began to expand their crops and partially forgo the fall hunt in order to concentrate on harvesting, the more traditional hunting families around them suddenly experienced less competition for game animals. That led to the perception—perhaps illusory—of lower population pressure in the hunting territories, which offered every incentive for these families to maintain their hunting-collecting way of life rather than turn to horticulture. In other words, the end of the Archaic period produced Southwestern families who lived side by side yet pursued very different daily economies.

Those economies were the equivalent of ecological niche separation: hunting-foraging territories versus farm plots, seed collecting in the uplands versus seed collecting at lower elevations. The two niches involved hugely different labor demands. Consequently, they involved different food intake needs and strikingly different family and reproductive dynamics. On the Pajarito Plateau, however, this niche separation was weak, because the plateau remained a prime place for both hunting and the foraging of acorns and piñon nuts, which horticulturalists still needed to supplement their small crops of carbohydrate-rich but protein-poor corn. People living on the plateau probably held on more tightly to their wild plant resources than did residents of the lowlands, which would explain the slower pace of horticultural development in Bandelier. Perhaps this is also why no early pithouse farmsteads have yet been found in the monument.

Evolution operates on variation. In humans, variation can be behavioral rather than genetic. That is why anthropologists make such a fuss over the concept of culture—it is a powerful behavioral mechanism that activates adaptation and evolution much more rapidly than genetic trends can. By the start of the common era or a few centuries earlier, we can see such behavioral variation in the U.S. Southwest. It shows up in on-the-ground archaeology in Bandelier National Monument and indeed all across the Southwest. That is the primary theme of the following chapter, in which it useful to remember that a horticultural family needs more food, more labor, more children, more storage, more precipitation, and less territory than a family that primarily hunts and secondarily forages. These needs lead to investment in structures (houses), infrastructure (farm plots), and artifacts (tools and pottery), all of which are visible archaeologically. Their archaeology is tangible evidence of greater energetic and caloric inputs. The greater a society's energetic power, the easier it is to see it on the ground.

Early Village Life

The Basketmaker and Pueblo I Periods

In northern New Mexico, the Basketmaker period spans the centuries from roughly the beginning of the common era through the 800s. It grew out of the En Medio period, and its beginnings were characterized by scattered hamlets of one to three dugout, log-and-dirt-roofed pithouses, an absence of pottery, and a consistently mixed economy. That economy included a good deal of wild plant collecting; the cultivation of corn, beans, and squash; and some hunting of large game, typically deer, antelope, and bighorn sheep. It is difficult to deduce the precise proportions of each component from ephemeral excavated remains, and the ratio probably varied by family, settlement, environmental location, and climatic conditions. Yet it is fairly safe to assert that horticulture contributed less than half the annual diet.

Richard Wetherill, the famous nineteenth-century rancher and explorer of Mesa Verde and Chaco Canyon, first used the name "Basketmaker" to describe the people and culture dating to the very early common era whose remains he found in Grand Gulch, Utah. There, sophisticated native artisans made spectacular baskets and woven goods of all kinds. The Basketmakers were by no means the first weavers, but they used dry caves for storage, which ensured that some of their textiles and basketry would be preserved. Archaeologists have found many examples of their elaborate sandals, yucca-fiber baskets, and netlike carrying bags in protected rock overhangs. The Basketmakers also were farmers, judging from the small corncobs they stored in granaries made of mud and rough masonry under dry rock overhangs.

Bandelier National Monument and the southern Pajarito uplands hold little evidence of Basketmaker-style, cliff-face storage areas, woven goods, or early pithouses (which in any case are difficult to locate visually). But numerous stone tools from the Basketmaker period (locally called the Developmental period), including some obsidian dart and lance points, have been found there, and modest Basketmaker farmsteads of up to three pithouses apiece have been excavated in adjacent lowlands along the Rio Grande, the

An early Basketmaker basket, a typical artifact used before pottery was made in northern New Mexico, or before 300 CE. Photograph by Blair Clark, 1989. Courtesy Museum of New Mexico, Utah collection, catalog number 43937/11.

Rio Puerco, and Jemez Creek. In the 1970s, archaeologists excavated a site called Ojalá Cave in Bandelier Monument, near the margins of Cochiti Reservoir. Although they found no pithouses there, they did uncover evidence that the rock overhang had been inhabited sporadically over a span of twenty-five hundred years, from middle Archaic to Basketmaker times. They also unearthed a large variety of stone tools and ancient seeds from plants collected nearby and eaten there. The latter find, along with animal bones from the cave, revealed a surprisingly sophisticated knowledge of seasonally available plants and animals. It tells us again that wild food harvests continued to be important even after corn was introduced.

A hundred miles northwest of Bandelier, in the so-called Navajo Reservoir district, pre-pottery Basketmaker sites can be found on mesas at six thousand feet or so in elevation. They are characterized by relatively large pithouses with antechambers, wide, surrounding aprons of cobbles, both interior and exterior storage pits, a tool kit dominated by stone grinding implements, and basketry. The cobbles surrounding the pithouses, rather like the stones that made up the ubiquitous fieldstone walls of colonial New England, probably came from small garden plots cleared in rocky, shallow drainages below the pithouse farmsteads. The cobble aprons are probably remnants of an ancient cooking technique in which people placed heated rocks in water held in pine-pitch-covered baskets in order to bring the water to a boil. The cobbles might also have served as heat sinks around the houses to help keep them warm during cold winters and as convenient ammunition to be hurled in case of attack.

By the mid-fourth century CE, people in the Navajo Reservoir district were using a brown pottery, today called Sambrito Brown—the first pottery known to have been made in northern New Mexico. (Despite the onset of pottery making at this time, archaeologists continue to call the people of the northern Southwest for several more centuries "Basketmakers.") Meanwhile, cobble aprons around pithouses disappeared. With the adoption of pottery, the stone boiling method presumably died out, because the direct transfer of heat from coals in a shallow hearth to a round-bottomed pot dramatically reduced both the amount of fuel and the time needed to cook plant foods. In short, pottery was highly efficient relative to earlier cooking methods. It greatly reduced the energy losses that were built into an ancient, multistep cooking process in which a great deal of heat was lost at each stage.

Sambrito Brown pottery, used only briefly, is rare enough that many field archaeologists have never seen it. And because such brown wares are supposed to be the signature of southern New Mexico's Mogollon culture, its presence in the north confounds some researchers. Pottery came to southern New Mexico first, however, as an imported technology from what is now old Mexico, in the 200s CE. Sambrito Brown merely marks the arrival of pottery in the Four Corners area from the south at about 325 to 350. By the late 300s and early 400s, local innovations in firing techniques, together with differences in the mineral contents of local clays, created the more typical gray wares by which the Puebloan peoples of the northern Southwest are recognized.

The earliest "signature" gray pottery made in northern New Mexico was a plain, undecorated ware called Lino Gray. Its gray paste color was a hallmark of ancestral Pueblo society for more than a thousand years. In the earliest pithouses it is occasionally found mixed with some of the brown clay cooking pots typical of the Mogollon people to the south (although neither pottery style has been found in Bandelier Monument itself). Archaeologists have never agreed about why these two fundamentally different pottery types appear together during this early period.

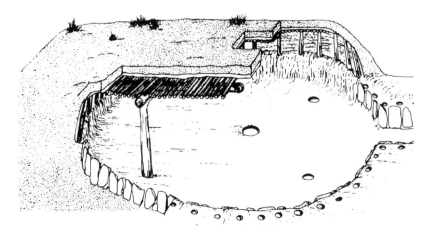

Artist's conception of a Basketmaker pithouse. Reproduced from *Prehistory of the Southwest*, by Linda Cordell. Courtesy Academic Press, Inc.

Like pottery, the Basketmaker pithouse was a manifestation of efficiency. Just two or three people could create one in a week to ten days. First, they loosened the earth with fire-hardened digging sticks and crude stone hoes. Then they removed it with trough-shaped, rectangular cottonwood scoops. Central support posts—often four of them—were then cut and set. The cribbed dome roof was first timbered (cutting the timbers with stone axes was the toughest work) and then "shingled" with saplings, bark, and boughs. Finally, it was covered with the excavated soil and then a layer of finer clay, if clay was available. As a last construction step, most floors were carefully leveled, some to be covered with a thin layer of slurried clay to create a smooth, sealed surface. Sometimes the builders used animal blood as a binder in the final floor surface.

The floor-level temperature of a yard-deep pithouse, roofed with four to six inches of dirt, would have varied by only four to seven degrees annually from a mean temperature of about sixty-nine degrees Fahrenheit, depending on elevation above sea level. Warm in winter and cool in summer, pithouses were as efficient as any modern, "green" earth-bermed dwelling. At elevations of five thousand to seventy-five hundred feet, where Basketmaker pithouses are most commonly found, no interior hearth was needed to keep the inhabitants warm. Indeed, the early pithouses found just outside of Bandelier Monument sometimes have no interior hearth. Many do have exterior ones—unsurprisingly, considering the discomfort of keeping a cooking fire burning indoors during a hot Southwestern summer.

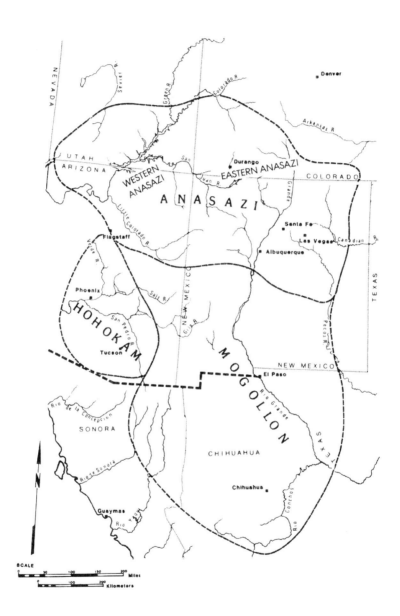

The ancestral Pueblo (Anasazi), Hohokam, and Mogollon regions in the
U.S. Southwest. Reproduced from *Prehistory of the Southwest*, by Linda Cordell.
Courtesy Academic Press, Inc.

As Basketmaker people settled into village life, the pace of development differed from one region to another, probably because of differences in local ecology, weather patterns, and population density. While the southern Pajarito apparently lingered in the mixed economic mode of an earlier age, powerful technological and demographic forces generated radical changes in village size, architecture, and regional economics elsewhere. Distinctive regional cultures began to develop in the Southwest, among them the Mogollon culture of southwestern New Mexico, with its signature pottery tradition, and the irrigation-based Hohokam society of southern Arizona. More important for the Bandelier story, the basin land and mesas surrounding Chaco Canyon, home to many long-established Basketmaker villages, saw the subsequent rise of Chaco Puebloan society.

Among the farmers of the San Juan Basin—the present-day Four Corners area—and northwestern New Mexico, village culture began to develop in earnest about 300 to 400 CE as the earlier, scattered pithouses of the pre-pottery Basketmaker years gave way to clusters of larger, deeper pithouses with built-in fire pits, ramp entrances (usually facing east to catch the morning sun), larger interior storage bins, and subfloor storage pits. The first sizable clusters of such pithouse farmsteads were established primarily in well-watered areas near the mountains surrounding the San Juan Basin. Soon afterward, in the late 400s and 500s, similar settlements were founded throughout the San Juan Basin and adjacent country in scattered areas of rich, organic soil (usually the clayey loams) with nearby seasonal streams, springs, or marshy areas. More modest versions of the Four Corners area settlements ringed the Pajarito Plateau at elevations averaging five thousand to six thousand feet. As noted, no pithouses of the 400s to 500s have been discovered in Bandelier Monument itself, so we do not know whether its Basketmaker inhabitants participated in the experimentation that led to the first settled horticultural villages found to the northwest and south.

It was the western half of the Chaco country that experienced the most remarkable growth during the next five or six centuries. Pithouse villages grew to as many as fifty to one hundred dwellings during the late Basketmaker period in places such as Skunk Springs, at the edge of the Chuska Valley near the present New Mexico–Arizona boundary. The most impressive of these villages were situated on mesas and low rises above good farmland, adjacent to mountainous areas offering large game, piñon nuts, and spring snowmelts that ensured water and enough recharge of soil moisture to promote the germination of seed corn.

In the Southwest, elevation and directional exposure largely determine local climate. The Pajarito Plateau may have been too high and had too short a growing season to enable people to produce large crops at this time. It likely took many centuries to adapt larger-cobbed corn, beans, and squash, first brought from Mexico, to the cool uplands of northern New Mexico. Cold nighttime temperatures and short growing seasons there required special crop varieties and planting techniques in order for horticulture to flourish.

Another intriguing possibility exists to explain the apparent dearth of Basketmaker-style pithouse villages on the Pajarito Plateau. Along with a large triangle of mountainous northern New Mexico that was also relatively "unsettled," the plateau might have been inhabited by people who clung to the seed-and-nut collecting and hunting way of life long after people in the San Juan Basin came to rely on corn, beans, squash, and small game. In other words, for centuries the mountains might have separated early peoples into emerging regional subcultures with different daily economies. Failure to achieve the same degree of niche separation in the daily Pajarito food economy that prevailed in northwestern New Mexico altered the pace and direction of development on the plateau for centuries.

The behaviors that accompany horticulture, as we have seen, include working harder, having more children, and placing a premium on storage. Farmers are also motivated to try to secure exclusive rights to good farmland. In places such as the U.S. Southwest, where rain falls unevenly on the landscape, farmers tend to adopt varied horticultural practices, which reduces their risk of failing to harvest a crop. They may also establish trade relationships with their neighbors, who might be able to supply food when harvests are abundant in one area but not another. In contrast, people who primarily hunt and forage, even if some families casually tend small plots of corn or beans, have little inducement to increase their labor, do not need to own land, and typically have fewer children. In short, the intensive horticulture economy of western New Mexico invited rapid change, larger settlements, higher birth rates, and continual experimentation in order to find incremental efficiencies: larger corn, better tools, proper fallowing intervals, astute crop watering techniques, and so forth. A modified Archaic- and early Basketmaker-style foraging economy placed a lesser premium on horticultural change. Societies practicing such an economy grow or evolve much more slowly than their farming counterparts. And this appears—barring new archaeological revelations—to have characterized the Pajarito Plateau during the first six or seven centuries of western New Mexico's accelerating village development.

The possibility that people on the Pajarito Plateau remained more typically Archaic than Basketmaker during the early village period cannot yet be either proved or disproved. But the clues are tantalizing. For one thing, pottery remained scarce throughout the mountainous triangle of the northern Rio Grande until about 600 to 900 CE. For another, the plateau inhabitants apparently took no part in the far-flung pottery trade that flourished to the west. Virtually none of the finely decorated black-on-white pottery made in western New Mexico from the late fifth through eighth centuries has been found in these highlands. Is it conceivable that in all those centuries, not one person came to the Polvadera quarry or Obsidian Ridge bearing a painted bowl to exchange for obsidian? If not, how did outsiders obtain Jemez Mountain obsidian, as we know they did? The rarity of outside trade goods on the Pajarito Plateau—indeed, of any evidence of economic connections with the vibrant Chacoan society to the west—remains puzzling, but it helps support the notion that this forested region was inhabited by "highlanders" who, for fundamental environmental reasons, remained stubbornly indifferent to the early settled farmers of the surrounding basins.

Further support comes from the pithouses that people carved into grassy knolls in an area known as the Gallina highlands, a bit northwest of Bandelier between present-day Cuba and Lindrith, New Mexico, during the seventh through tenth centuries. These large, deep pithouses, often as many as a dozen of them tucked into a narrow meadow, and the artifacts found in them, display few of the distinguishing characteristics that archaeologists associate with early Chacoan society. These part-time upland farmers of small-cobbed corn hunted along the west flanks of the Jemez Mountains and made a distinctive pottery. Their stone tools did not closely mirror the changes taking place to the west. These villagers probably engaged in little external trade, since almost no early Chacoan pottery is found in their villages, and none of theirs appears in early Chacoan sites. In other words, they seem to have been every bit as isolated in their bastion of traditional lifeways as the families of the Pajarito apparently were.

In addition, the Gallina-area villages were separated from the northeast frontier of Chacoan development by a desolate no-man's land lacking permanent villages of any kind. Relative to Bandelier, this uninhabited frontier lay to the northwest, running along the southwestern flank of the densely settled Chaco country. Even at the zenith of Chacoan power in the late eleventh century, part of this no-man's land contained only ephemeral, scattered campsites. Because of this geographical separation, some archaeologists see the Pajarito inhabitants as the southern tip of a great wedge of local mountain peoples who did not participate in Chacoan development during the early common era. Horticulture in the mountains seems to have been relatively casual, produced spotty rewards, and probably never overshadowed hunting and foraging until the eleventh to sixteenth centuries. Just how much farming took place in Bandelier Monument during the centuries from 400 to 800 CE remains unanswered.

There is even some question about whether these mountain folk were closely related genetically to the western New Mexico Chacoans at all. Studies of skeletal remains, some of them done sketchily more than half a century ago, hint that the mountains of northern New Mexico were a biological as well as a cultural barrier. The scanty data currently available preclude a definite answer, as does my profession's unfathomable failure to exploit DNA analysis more consistently to resolve such issues.

Throughout the Chaco country, sufficient social and architectural changes took place during the late Basketmaker period that archaeologists perceive it as having given way, around 700 or 800 CE, to a new era, the time of the ancestral Pueblo Indians. Pithouses became smaller and more rectangular, and their internal layout passed beyond the experimental stage to become standardized. Outdoor ramadas (branch lean-tos) and cooking areas became common, and some villages had modest plazas. Storage pits dug into the floors of pithouses grew larger and more elaborate. But they still tended to become damp during late winter snowmelts, which ruined the seed corn, so people began replacing them with small, above-ground, stone storage rooms erected outside their pithouses. To archaeologists, it is these above-ground storage rooms that announce the earliest Puebloan years, which they label "Pueblo I."

In most of the bigger villages in the Four Corners country, residents built one or more large, dugout earth lodges. Archaeologists generally describe these as kivas or proto-kivas, predecessors of the circular ceremonial chambers dug into Tyuonyi's great plaza at Bandelier nearly eight centuries later. Judging from the range of artifacts found in excavated ones, residents of late Basketmaker and Pueblo I hamlets used their large dugout structures as community chambers as well as for sacred rituals. Over time, then, we see a progression from circular family pithouses to large pithouse–community structures and then to proto-kivas, which metamorphosed, finally, into more exclusively religious chambers.

People in the larger and economically more dominant settled villages of western New Mexico generally owned much larger quantities of fine, painted pottery than did their poorer neighbors to the east, in the northern Rio Grande area. Precious ornaments and exotic trade goods became increasingly common in the San Juan Basin villages. Spondylus shell was imported from the Gulf of California, eight hundred miles to the southwest. Artisans chopped it into rough discs and ground their edges smooth, forming circular beads of a kind now called heishi. New Mexico's Pueblo Indians still make fine heishi, prized by Indian, Hispanic, and Anglo buyers alike. First, holes are drilled in hundreds of the rough shell chips. In the historic past, these chips were then strung on long strands of yucca fiber; now, it is usually fine cord or fishing line. Traditionally, the strands of chips were then tediously hand rolled between two rough sandstone slabs and ground into exquisitely delicate beads. Today the work is usually done by machine-driven grinders.

Early Pueblo ornament makers also fashioned small pendants and beads from imported coral, jet, freshwater shells from Texas, and pipestone from what is now Pipestone National Monument in Minnesota. All these materials found their way to the Southwest in modest quantities during the 700s to 900s CE. Another regional stone for heishi-like strung discs, though a less preferred one, was the banded gray shale found in the Chaco country's Bisti Badlands. Pieces of the shale were chipped and ground in the same way as the more valuable imported shell.

Turquoise, too, was traded west into the Chaco heartland. Some of it came from deposits near the present-day village of Cerrillos, New Mexico, southeast of Santa Fe, which are still being worked today. Although native people were mining Cerrillos turquoise with stone tools at least as early as the 900s CE, the mines reached their first heyday in the high Chacoan decades of the mid-eleventh century. The largest open mine continued to produce high-grade gem material for native peoples into the early 1600s, when Spaniards took control and enlarged it. From the late 1800s to the 1930s it was owned by Tiffany Jewelers of New York. In 2010, a portion of the old diggings was being operated as the family-owned Casa Grande Trading Company in the village of Cerrillos.

Besides establishing a trade in exotic goods, members of the San Juan Basin's growing communities had, through selective breeding, developed

Sandstone manos and trough-shaped metates from a Chaco Canyon ruin. The large grinding surfaces on these implements, used for grinding corn into meal, were very efficient relative to earlier ones. Courtesy National Park Service, Bandelier National Monument.

corn plants that likely produced more ears of large-cobbed corn than those their ancestors had known. These plants generated larger, more consistent yields. Farmers now laid out their garden plots more carefully, sometimes bordering them with low rock walls to slow runoff, so that precious rainwater could be absorbed by the thin desert soil.

Farming and food processing implements also evolved as the Basket-maker way of life transformed itself into the Pueblo way. Hafted stone and antler hoes became more sophisticated. Long gone were the small, one-hand manos and small, flat metates, which had been replaced by noticeably larger, more elaborate, elongated manos and trough-shaped metates made in several grades of coarseness. By the dawn of the 800s, householders sometimes lined these grinding tools up in rows of two or three stones of coarse, medium, and fine grit, inside special rooms. There, women and girls ground large quantities of dried corn and a variety of wild grass seeds, which they still went out to collect, turning them into meal.

By Pueblo I times, large pithouse villages with elaborate aboveground storage rooms dotted the windy mesas of the San Juan Basin. Social, religious, and economic life had become much more complex during the half-millennium since fired pottery was introduced into what is now northwestern New Mexico. To be sure, people still made some of their old, intricate woven goods of enduring utility, such as yucca-fiber sandals, seed-collecting baskets, and cloaks made of turkey feathers entwined with strips of rabbit fur. To these they added finely woven sashes of native cotton imported from Arizona or southern New Mexico. The primary trade items across the San Juan Basin and its margins, however, were now a half-dozen varieties of finely painted black-on-white ceramic bowls. In nearly every village, potters also produced well-made ollas for storage, cooking, and carrying water, either leaving the surfaces of the vessels plain or pinching the clay coils into a corrugated appearance. Some large, particularly fine ollas were traded over distances of thirty to seventy miles.

The hallmarks of the Pueblo I period were rapid growth in village size, somewhat increased social and religious complexity, expanding trade networks for regional products such as seed corn, black-on-white bowls, and Jemez obsidian, and even more labor-intensive forms of horticulture. Innovation reached a peak relative to earlier times. These hallmarks are all keys to rising energy or caloric flows through San Juan Basin society. When societies grow rapidly and become more complex, they consume calories and raw materials voraciously. They must produce, for example, ever larger harvests and more pottery. They must also balance their increasing consumption with new, incremental efficiencies (larger-cobbed corn; more organized labor; better, more efficient tools) to subsidize an increased rate of growth. They had to find and establish new, premium, naturally well-watered farm plots and innovate in crop varieties. As growing populations expanded their horticulture into drier land with poorer soil adjacent to their older farming districts, they had to develop devices to control the flow of water and divert it onto their fields.

People's finding, using, and altering new living and farming places— an efficiency necessity in the 800s to early 900s CE—accounts in part for the rapid geographic expansion archaeologists see in the remains of farmsteads and farm plots over large swaths of the southern and west-central San Juan Basin during this time. Usually, researchers credit population growth for this change. That was certainly a factor, but it might have been less important than the need to expand district-wide farm production in places that, if modified, allowed for maximized horticultural output at bearable labor costs. If farming is hard work, then farming poor, unproductive soil over a deep water table is even more work—at a lower return.

Woven yucca-fiber sandals. Such sandals, in many variations, were a staple of Southwestern life from Archaic times into the nineteenth century. Photograph by Wyatt Davis, 1940. Courtesy Museum of New Mexico, negative number 43934.

Turkey feather blanket. These thermally efficient blankets were used in one form or another in the northern Southwest for more than a thousand years. Photograph by Blair Clark, 1989. Courtesy Museum of New Mexico, catalog number 46043/11.

White Mound–La Plata Black-on-white bowl, late Basketmaker period, northern
New Mexico. This kind of pottery was typical during the early expansion of ancestral
Pueblo trade networks in the 500s to 700s CE. Courtesy Michael P. Marshall, Maxwell
Museum Collections.

Later farming expansions to the west of the Pajarito Plateau during
Chaco's high period (950–1090 CE) were often "infill" moves to much less
desirable planting locations with poorer soils and lower water tables. This
strategy led to a combination of greater labor investment and smaller crop
yields. It shouts across the centuries that growth was out of control, common labor was becoming less valuable, and the efficiency strategy was actually
a short-term stopgap. As I show in the next chapter, the consequences of
that inefficient dynamic profoundly affected late-period Chacoan society.
It is a dynamic that still cyclically affects the economy and job market of
the United States today.

To all current knowledge, the area in and around Bandelier National
Monument continued to lag in these developments, and the district's few

surrounding settlements remained small and scattered. But by the tenth century, the late Basketmaker and subsequent Pueblo I people of the Chaco country had set in motion irreversible forces that would fundamentally transform ancient Southwestern society. They were the same forces that are still transforming contemporary America—that is, the dual stratagem of increasing energy inputs while finding or inventing new efficiencies. This delicate balancing act determined the course of the next few centuries as Chacoan society went into a growth overdrive.

Power, Complexity, and Failure

The Chaco Period

Across the northern Southwest, the era of pithouse villages ended in a whirlwind of change. During the six centuries of Basketmaker and Pueblo I development, the number of settlements in the San Juan Basin had increased roughly tenfold. The next tenfold increase would take place in just two centuries, from roughly 900 to 1100 CE, a tripling of the rate of growth. With that tripling would come a breathtaking increase in annual energy or calorie flows: more work, more farmsteads, more corn, more babies, and, eventually, more complexity. With more complexity came more costs.

At the very beginning of the Basketmaker period, villages had been situated on mesas or hugged the mountains, where there was access to upland hunting. By the end of that period—between 700 and 800 CE, depending on locality—several thousand settlements lay scattered across the San Juan Basin, in virtually every place that offered rich soil and dependable water. A number of late Pueblo I villages situated on the margins of lower-elevation valleys apparently no longer claimed access to the old upland hunting districts. And judging from the proliferation of villages featuring arcs of above-ground storerooms, horticultural production had grown.

As a consequence, population began to increase rapidly between the ninth and tenth centuries, and new styles of village construction appeared. In one style, existing Pueblo I storerooms were renovated into small blocks of stone masonry or wattle-and-daub (jacal) residential rooms, and the former family pithouses were shifted to use in community and religious functions. At Chaco Canyon, such late Pueblo I renovations were particularly common. Three notable renovations of late Pueblo I settlements in Chaco Canyon added huge, outsized masonry storage rooms. Each of the three villages—Peñasco Blanco, Una Vida, and Pueblo Bonito—guarded entrances to the canyon, and together they had begun to metamorphose into the earliest known masonry great houses by the late 800s. From that time forward, raw storage capacity and village size went hand in hand.

Nearly simultaneously, about eighty miles to the southwest, small, rectangular blocks of above-ground masonry rooms appeared in the Red Mesa

The Chaco site of El Faro. As Chaco Canyon slipped into crisis mode in the late eleventh or early twelfth century, this compact, fortified complex was built atop a dramatic butte overlooking a man-made causeway called the North Road, which stretched from the canyon to the San Juan River country.

Red Mesa Black-on-white jar. Red Mesa Black-on-white was the hall-mark ceramic of the early Chaco period, the 800s to early 1000s CE. Courtesy Michael P. Marshall, Maxwell Museum Collections.

Valley, near present-day Gallup, New Mexico. Along with them came a new way of decorating black-on-white pottery. Named for the place where it was first found, Red Mesa Black-on-white was painted with an iron-oxide-based mineral pigment instead of the plant-based carbon pigments that artists had used until that time. By 950, Red Mesa Black-on-white pottery had spread across the southern San Juan Basin and into the lower elevations of the Cochiti–Santa Fe district. Nearly a century later, a wave of vibrant economic activity had carried these traded ceramics as far north as Taos, New Mexico, and as far east as the Watrous Valley on the edge of northeastern New Mexico's plains. That economic wave is now known as the "Chaco phenomenon."

The dynamics of early Chacoan expansion appear to have been two-pronged. One arm was the macroeconomic "market" response, as exemplified by the huge storerooms built in the mid-800s. The other was the microeconomic level of adaptive change—that is, the family-level dynamic—which is even more fascinating. As early as the second decade of the 800s, major changes in land use began in the area just east of modern Gallup. There, some families moved away from the Pueblo I settlements along the edges of the Red Mesa Valley and built small, above-ground masonry farmsteads in the valley itself.

In effect, the people of the Gallup area, like their ancestors, were engaging in what ecologists and biologists might think of as "niche separation" in their horticultural strategies and use of the landscape. Valley margins, mesa tops above them, and valley floors were all in use at once. And in each niche, different but contemporaneous architecture and pottery defy the tidy, normative time-period classifications of traditional Southwestern archaeology. This niche separation proceeded rapidly, because humans adapt primarily through cultural behavior. That strategy is sometimes risky (we get it wrong almost as often as we get it right), but culture bypasses the slow, genetically driven pace of adaptation left to other species.

The rapid pace of change from the mid-800s to the mid-900s created an extraordinarily complex archaeological record. In several of the upland areas encircling the San Juan Basin, Red Mesa Black-on-white bowls were traded into Pueblo I and even late Basketmaker-style settlements, where pithouses continued to be inhabited. In the lowlands of the Red Mesa Valley, pithouse construction, which had characterized both the Basketmaker and Pueblo I periods, ceased. There, well-constructed pueblos of tabular sandstone, with eight to twenty rooms each, were erected in an accelerating frenzy of construction. Obviously, cultivating larger-cobbed corn in the best-watered locations at lower elevations, with their longer growing seasons, worked. Occasionally, new pueblos were built directly on top of old pithouses. In a few cases, people halted the construction of nearly complete pithouses, filled in the gaping holes, and built masonry rooms above them. But most of these new-style, above-ground sandstone pueblos were sited where no permanent settlement preceded them. Archaeologists refer to these masonry farmsteads as defining the Pueblo II period, but they are in fact the hallmark of *early* Pueblo II, which overlaps the end of both Basketmaker III and Pueblo I pithouse communities in the Gallup district.

In and around the Red Mesa Valley, a few pithouse hamlets remained in use for a generation or two but then were abandoned as even more families poured into the area to pursue intensive farming. Other pithouses were remodeled into kivas, becoming architecturally more distinctive—and

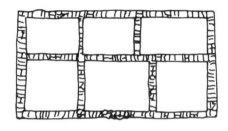

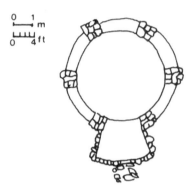

Plan of a typical Red Mesa Valley house block of the 800s and 900s CE, a small, rectangular, sandstone pueblo adjacent to a pithouse "kiva." Reproduced from *Prehistory of the Southwest*, by Linda Cordell. Courtesy Academic Press, Inc.

probably more sacred—as ordinary pithouses generally disappeared from the fifteen thousand square miles of the central San Juan Basin. No longer was it important to situate villages right against the mountains, for access to hunting. The focus of economic activity across the region shifted to drier, scrubby basin land. For more than two centuries, during the ensuing Chaco period, daily survival in the farmsteads depended heavily on growing large-cobbed corn, raising domesticated turkeys, hunting very small game animals, and collecting local wild plants.

In the southern San Juan Basin, nearly all these changes during the early Pueblo II period appear to have been generated by family-driven economic decisions. Many of those decisions led to greater energy investments. Constructing an above-ground masonry pueblo of eight to ten rooms required much more labor and material than did building several pithouses sufficient to house the same population. The stone pueblos were also more difficult to cool and heat. The expansion of horticultural fields required many more hours of heavy labor, and hunting small game is calorically much more costly, in proportion to returns, than hunting large animals. In short, these settlements were calorically expensive relative to the earlier pithouse villages, with their mixed economies.

Offsetting these high calorie costs were increased efficiencies gained by harvesting larger-cobbed corn, raising turkeys, using water control devices, employing ever-evolving grinding stones and other tools, and continuing to supplement the food supply with some foraging. Domesticated turkeys probably had a twofold effect in early Pueblo II society. First, they efficiently converted garden waste into meat as they foraged on insects and invasive weeds. Second, and more important, the females laid eggs rich in both fat and protein. Those eggs would have been an ideal additive to a gruel made from ground corn or yucca meal and used as a pabulum to supplement breast milk. The added nutrients might have contributed to infant survival, a possibility that would be easy to test by analyzing burial data from a dozen or so medium-size, early Pueblo II settlements, some of which had more turkey bones and pens than others. Even a small percentage decrease in infant mortality would have translated, like the effects of compound interest, into a significant population increase over the course of a century.

Chaco Canyon itself experienced a version of the early Pueblo II period very different from that of the Red Mesa Valley. While the world beyond the canyon walls was transformed, few Chaco farmers abandoned their Pueblo I-style architecture of pithouses and above-ground storerooms. But an emerging elite there began to create outsized versions of villages built in the Pueblo I style, versions that eventually became the Chacoan great houses so often written about. The Chaco era, then, encompassed two stories: one about Chaco Canyon and the other about the growing number of farms in the basin land beyond the canyon walls. The development of those far-flung farms determined the pace of change during Chaco's early days, the 800s and 900s CE. At that time, Chaco did not nurture the Pueblo II farmers of the San Juan Basin; rather, they fed Chaco.

Rainfall during those centuries, though not particularly abundant, was somewhat more stable from year to year than it had been between 750 and 850 CE. Even this tiny increase in predictability, coupled with still available pockets of good soil atop shallow water tables, had already allowed the Red Mesa Valley farmers to expand into previously unused countryside. A similar expansion spread to other parts of the San Juan Basin before 1000, when many hundreds, if not thousands, of small pueblos began to be built on less-preferred soils throughout the southern basin, in places where no prior pithouse village had existed.

This second surge in basin-land farm creation meant higher labor costs, somewhat lower crop yields, and huge regional investments in the infrastructure of houses and new fields. It is unlikely that such a costly frenzy of horticultural expansion would have taken place had precipitation patterns not become much more predictable. That greater predictability lasted for the better part of a century, the 1000s, during which many Chacoan farmers pioneered dry-farming techniques in risky, less-protected basin settings. Others pushed eastward toward the Rio Grande. The increased predictability of precipitation coincided with both the greatest growth surge of Chaco society and the taking of increased risks.

Despite the increased energy costs of the settlement surge, new horticultural efficiencies and a pattern of farming the clayey loam soils deposited in pockets on the valley floors fueled a rapid increase in the construction of new Pueblo II masonry farmsteads. Hamlets began to appear in virtually every locality along the western and southern margins of the San Juan Basin. This surge in housing starts probably reached its first peak in the 950s to 970s. But as is so often the case in human societies, the Chacoans' rapid growth, coupled with a resumption of patchy and variable rainfall in the late 900s, overwhelmed the efficiencies that had sustained their way of life for nearly a century. The archaeological evidence is still spotty, but in both the Red Mesa Valley and among the farmsteads in Chaco Canyon itself, there is evidence of scattered violence: partly burned structures, human long bones pierced by dart or lance shafts, and blunt trauma fractures in skulls. In more remote areas, small, stockaded settlements also hint at social tensions.

More important, severe malnutrition is widely detectable in the bones of people buried at the farmsteads in the late 900s. A larger proportion of infants and young children were buried at this time, which in itself is a sign of poor nutrition. The bones of children and adults alike are often thin and brittle, and in what constitutes the most compelling evidence, analysts see gray, enamel-poor, striated bands in the front teeth of adults who were buried late in this time period. These gray bands, caused by episodes of near catastrophic malnutrition, show that repeated episodes of near starvation took place during these people's infancy and early childhood in the 960s to 980s, in both Chaco Canyon and several outlying areas.

This interruption in the century-long growth of basin-land farming required the San Juan Basin people to restrategize, rewire their trading patterns, and find new efficiencies. Under these circumstances, Chacoans living in the canyon's largest, most prosperous Pueblo I–style farmsteads, who had been trading heavily in pottery and other items for a century or more, apparently took the lead in organizing trade and innovating in infrastructure. They enlarged several trunk roads that had begun as footpaths several centuries earlier, increased the number and sizes of their storerooms, and better organized trade between the plateau country to the north and northwest of Chaco Canyon and the struggling Red Mesa Valley farming district to the south. As noted, good fortune favored the Chacoans as precipitation again became increasingly reliable after 1000 CE, and the steps they took proved hugely successful. By the end of the tenth century, innovation had shifted from the outlying farmsteads to the Chaco Canyon great houses and their elites. Decisions were becoming more centralized, rather than being determined primarily by trends among thousands of small farmers.

Just after 1000, farmsteads covered all but a rough arc along the northeastern edge of the San Juan Basin. Numerous races of corn, several varieties of premodern pinto beans, squash, melons, pigweed, and native grasses such as Indian rice grass made up most of the diet. Meat came primarily from rabbits, domesticated turkeys, and even wood rats and gophers. Large game was scarce, although hunters occasionally took bighorn sheep, pronghorn antelope, and deer.

In the Bandelier area, to the east of the Chacoan world, people still quarried obsidian and turned it into darts and true arrowheads, which archaeologists find in the ruins of settlements along the Rio Grande's lower elevations. At some of these farmsteads, residents continued, anomalously, to build pithouses. Between present-day Española and Albuquerque, New Mexico, both pithouse villages and small masonry or adobe pueblos contain occasional traces of Chaco-period pottery. Microscopic grains of pollen from corn and other garden plants appear in soil samples taken at these sites. They also hold many more butchered bones of large animals than are found at contemporaneous sites in the western Chaco country.

Local trade seems to have connected villages from south to north along the Rio Grande. Even at the late date of 1000 to 1040 CE, decorated Mogollon pottery continued to be mixed with locally made cooking wares in the area between modern Bernalillo and Belen. By about 1050, however, Chacoan society had become an unprecedented force in the ancient Southwest. Enormous expansion took place at the old, large settlements in Chaco Canyon, in the Gallup area and on the north flanks of Mount

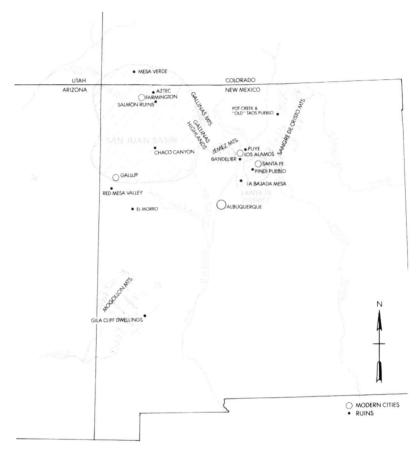

Late Chacoan and upland archaeological sites in the northern Southwest. Courtesy Mary Powell/Ancient City Press.

Taylor to the southeast, in the Chuska Valley, and along the lower Chaco River to the northwest of Chaco Canyon. Economic efficiencies promoted by Chaco elites were not just good business for them; they were the fuels that powered explosive growth.

As Chacoan economic power peaked between 1025 and 1075, new great houses functioned as huge trading and ceremonial villages for the region. Now called "outliers" because they lie outside Chaco Canyon itself, these structures featured large ground-floor rooms, beautifully banded, thick sandstone walls, pairs of kivas in their courtyards, and often two or three upper stories of many storerooms. The function of these sites is easily deduced from their rigidly formulaic inclusion of tremendous storage capacity and enormous ceremonial chambers. As in Chaco Canyon itself fifty years earlier, so in outlying places people took ancient footpaths that had connected long-established farmsteads and turned them into carefully finished roadways. Clusters of the oldest and largest farming villages—favored for natural growth by their good soil and water and almost always underlain by older pithouse villages—in the 1000s became magnets for new Chacoan great houses. These projects, most archaeologists agree, were engineered and organized by Chaco's elites.

Yet others of the great Chacoan "towns" had not even been built by the 1050s. The great kiva at Aztec Ruins National Monument; Salmon Ruins, near Bloomfield, New Mexico; Pueblo Pintado; and other late outliers on the margins of the Chaco heartland were built just after Chacoan society peaked in overall growth. After about 1075, Chacoan growth in one place was usually marked by a decline somewhere else. This, too, is reminiscent of economic patterns in the contemporary United States; we do have our rust belts. Chaco's late-eleventh-century pockets of decline most likely created "dust belts" as abandoned, dried-out fields simply blew away on the spring winds.

During this peak in the development and export of great houses, the Chacoans appear to have taken a formulaic approach that I call "roads, rituals, and great houses." In other words, they exported a complex combination of infrastructure and storage—and with it, the redistribution of corn and other products among villages—all wrapped in an increasingly lavish package of ritual.

By the mid-1000s the Chacoan economy, infrastructure, and ritual were, as in the late 800s to mid-900s, enlarging the geographic domain of Chaco Canyon once again. The elites in the canyon great houses drove logistics, ideology, and complexity, in addition to infrastructure, while the surrounding farmers drove basic food production. In farmsteads, a ratio of one unit of residential space to one unit of family storage never changed after 1000. Storage in the great houses, on the other hand, increased to a ratio of three units of storage to one unit of residential space by the mid-1000s. It is the architecture of exported great houses—a combination of storerooms and kivas with only modest residential space—that unequivocally connects storage capacity to ritual. Economy and religion were rapidly becoming inseparable halves of the Chaco Canyon elites' exported model. Eventually, the residents of the canyon great houses themselves may have become more engaged in the regular conduct of ritual, publicly emphasizing the canyon as a ceremonial center. But the great houses and their ceremonies could not have expanded in the mid- to late 1000s had their storerooms not been scattered across thirty thousand square miles. I think of this as a bit like Washington, D.C., where congressmen and senators make C-SPAN speeches about democracy and freedom in a grand setting, even as the defense-related economics of their districts form the day's real business. Both Chacoan economy and religion were connected, in turn, to an increasingly elaborate road system that, in the mid-1000s, connected all the great houses to Chaco Canyon. This, too, has a familiar ring to it.

After 1050 or so, Chacoan growth and complexity changed in pace, tone, and detail. The hallmark of these changes is the huge but episodic renovation projects undertaken in Chaco Canyon between the 1060s and the first decade of the 1100s. Some such projects focused on adding new residential wings to canyon great houses or adding kivas and more upper-story rooms at outliers. Other projects concentrated on building new, even wider roadways beyond the canyon. Some of these late, lavish roadways make more interpretive sense as avenues to ritual destinations than as basic means of efficient transport intended to maximize regional trade. Finally, many more new kivas were carved out of old great-house plazas than had ever existed before. It is as if the "roads, rituals, and great houses" formula had been carried to excess, becoming a knee-jerk obsession rather than a considered response to necessity. One sees parallels almost daily in the news today: "Drill, baby, drill!" and "Cut taxes and deregulate markets to grow this economy!" Both of these modern mantras are about power, to the exclusion of balancing efficiencies.

The late Chacoan period was the time when the most elaborate wall structures, pottery, ritual, regalia, grave offerings, and exotic goods were also produced. If the demands of ritual tied to growing, planting, and selecting corn increased as the numbers and sizes of kivas increased, then it is plausible to infer that Chacoan priests and elites also took more control over farm production—not just infrastructural changes—in the 1000s. Such a change might have shifted decisions even more dramatically away from the farmers who had pioneered horticultural expansion and away from their concept of "efficient market frontiers," which modern free-market economists still hold dear. In effect, such changes might have been similar to recent historic attempts at central planning in large societies. Russia, China, and Cuba are often named as examples. Ideological labeling aside, the most important consequence of such a change would have been the destruction of information conduits between producers (farmers) and planners (great-house elites). Such a "disconnect" has high risk written all over it. Just ask a laid-off veteran assembly-line worker from General Motors or Chrysler what happens when management becomes disengaged from labor, begins to assume that its workers are dunce-like "little people," and as a by-product loses all practical touch with its consumers and its production process. Such disconnections usually lead to unhappy results.

The fabulous Chaco phenomenon of the mid- to late 1000s marked the zenith of Pueblo II society, which was followed by a final, elite-driven expansion that left awesome buildings (usually labeled Pueblo III) for us to admire. The immense sandstone structures created during the zenith in Chaco Canyon itself, together with outliers such as Aztec Ruins and Salmon Ruins, were all erected in a span of about 140 years. Indeed, 43 percent of all the archaeological sites ever recorded in New Mexico were built between 950 and 1100 CE. Until the 1050s through 1070s, most of that growth was represented by ordinary Pueblo II farmsteads. This stunning growth was largely the result of the Chaco era.

In late Chacoan times, remarkable social, economic, architectural, and technological complexity replaced the raw geographical expansion of earlier boom years. And that complexity was elite driven. By 1100 the Chacoans had spread over more than fifty thousand square miles, an area about the size of Scotland. The number of their villages had increased almost tenfold over that of the late Basketmaker period. An estimated twenty thousand Chacoan farmsteads and nearly two hundred major "outlier," trade-and-ritual great houses were linked in a huge trade-food-transportation-ceremonial network.

Small margins of surplus corn from many thousands of modest farmsteads were needed to fuel the infrastructure necessary to incorporate diverse peoples and diverse trading districts into a functional whole. But Chacoan society had already begun to outgrow its agricultural underpinnings at a time when the need for even more efficient food distribution was increasing. Horticultural expansion onto poorer soils in places with suboptimal soil moisture, cold air pockets, and uncertain growing seasons meant that such lately colonized districts produced declining crop yields in return for greater labor and infrastructure costs. Expansion no longer guaranteed the efficiencies of scale that had been obtained fifty to seventy-five years earlier through horticultural technologies refined to succeed in areas of highly productive soils and favorable microclimates. Apparently, the prevailing

A mineral-painted Chaco Black-on-white mug dating to
about 1000 CE, from site BC 59 10/10. Courtesy Michael P.
Marshall, Maxwell Museum Collections.

organizational formula failed to account for changing circumstances. As
Chacoan growth shifted from being driven by farmers to being more balanced between farmers and planners and finally to being singularly driven
by planners or elites, it became more expensive and much more fragile.
The great bulk of participating Chacoan peoples actually began to experience a decline in living standards.

The Red Mesa Valley, one of Chaco's earliest and most reliable corn-
producing districts, had already begun to languish as its better soils were
depleted by two centuries of continuous harvesting. Corn depletes soil
nitrogen, something that is still a problem in contemporary agriculture.
Thus, the efficiency of growing corn, even in once-favored localities, was
in decline. Not surprisingly, an eleventh-hour push took place toward horticultural expansion as far east in New Mexico as the Pecos River valley.

But these large, scattered populations, which the Chaco road system
never effectively incorporated, suffered from inefficiencies of transportation and local food shortages. Archaeological evidence from the middle
Pecos Valley shows that as the first small waves of desperate farmers moved

out of the declining, overcrowded Red Mesa Valley, those who pioneered farmsteads on the eastern frontier in the late 1000s faced both new agricultural hardships and confrontations with hostile, non-Puebloan plains people, who were still primarily gatherers and hunters.

Small horticultural settlements also sprang up at this time in the middle Rio Grande Valley and in the Mora area to the northeast. They represent the greatest geographical spread of horticultural colonization until the 1700s, when Spanish farmers recolonized much of the upper Pecos Valley. Some of these ancient farmsteads combined a few shallow pithouses with adobe or wattle-and-daub, above-ground rooms. Two to six structures were common, and construction techniques tended toward the expedient—that is, the efficient. Local variations of gray pottery typically appear in these archaeological sites along with a combination of local black-on-white bowls and imports from elsewhere. The imports can include variants of Mogollon pottery from southwestern New Mexico; black-on-whites from farther south along the Rio Grande, between Albuquerque and Socorro; and scarce, late Chacoan black-on-whites. Plant and animal remains in these settlements point to a mixed economy similar to that of mid- to late Basketmaker times—the 400s to 600s CE —in the Four Corners country. Researchers find some corn and lots of gathered foodstuffs, including yuccas, agaves, mesquite, chokecherries, wolfberries, and all the productive grasses. Unlike in the core Chacoan world of the time, they also find bones of large game animals, showing that hunters in the east gained renewed access to such prey, including bison at the margins of the high plains of eastern New Mexico.

Other emigrants from the Chacoan core, including some from the Red Mesa Valley, began to move into uplands surrounding the San Juan Basin— the foothills of the Chuska and Zuni Mountains—as early as the mid-1000s. Although few in number, these people, too, built pithouses and pursued a mixed subsistence economy almost identical to that of their Basketmaker forebears. In both cases of relocation—to the San Juan uplands and to the Rio Grande and beyond—the archaeological evidence strongly implies a lifestyle refocused on low-intensity labor, low-cost construction, and life on a frontier with neither elaborate infrastructure nor elaborate social structure. In short, these people embraced efficiency and eschewed risk.

Meanwhile, by studying burial sites and associated human skeletons, archaeologists know that the entire regional economy centered on the Chaco core became increasingly fragile in late Chacoan times. One study estimated that infant mortality was nearly 50 percent among farmers in the Gallup area by roughly 1050 CE. (By contrast, when 2 percent of infants in any American locality die before one year of age, it is considered a public health crisis.) Human bones recovered from both the Red Mesa Valley and small Chacoan farmsteads right in Chaco Canyon show consistent evidence of the diminishing quality of life. Among the signatures are severe tooth decay, decreasing tooth size, skull deformities, osteoporosis, osteoarthritis, and declining body size and skeletal robustness.

Chacoan society, like our own, came to be based on growth and the lavish use of resources. And like ours, it was enormously successful but had its problems. Those problems fell most heavily on the food producers. Also like the modern United States, Chacoan society was probably an amalgamation of ethnic and language groups. Some archaeologists speculate that in the construction of several late Chacoan great houses, such as Pueblo Pintado, crews from different ethnic groups built adjacent masonry room blocks using different units of measurement. Today, half a dozen Pueblo language communities claim descent from Chaco—speakers of the Tiwa, Tewa, Towa, Keres, Zuni, and Hopi languages. Several of these communities have other, separate ritual languages that are kept unknown to outsiders and even to the uninitiated among themselves. Judging from similar realities in other parts of the world, these separate languages likely are relics tied to the most ancient and sacred rituals, highlighting ancient historical events. Such hidden languages could be testaments to little-studied historical complexity among these peoples' Chacoan ancestors. Perhaps the secret languages function for Pueblo Indians today much the way computer programming languages do for all of us. Though arcane to most people, they are critical to our daily information flows.

In any case, during the late eleventh century, problems created by rapid growth pushed the Chacoans into building wider, more elaborate roadways, adding more storerooms and kivas, and incurring ever greater costs to pump up their increasingly fragile regional society. Skilled masons built huge new great houses, such as Pueblo Pintado on Chaco Canyon's new southeast road to its eastern frontier. Judging from artifacts and site characteristics, this frontier separated Chacoan society from Gallina villagers of the northern Jemez district, whose ancestors had built the first Basketmaker-like pithouses there.

Pueblo Pintado, an immense pile of sandstone enclosing sixty huge ground-floor rooms, topped in places with second and third stories, was built largely in the winter of 1060–1061, quite like a magnificent, WPA-style project right out of the Roosevelt era. No single, dense cluster of farmsteads existed at this location previously, so Pueblo Pintado had only widely scattered pockets of farmers to serve administratively. Why did such an area require a district granary, a new roadway, and paired great kivas in which to conduct rituals, all constructed at enormous expense? The answer is not obvious. Neither is Pintado's "return on investment." This great house seems recognizable, though, in terms of modern American behavior: it has "stimulus project" written all over it.

Even more dramatic, by the early twelfth century Salmon Ruins and Aztec Ruins, far to the north on the San Juan and Animas Rivers, respectively, had been built on the model of Chaco Canyon's high-period, rectangular great houses and incorporated into the Chacoan economic sphere. By the 1080s to early 1100s, people at these sites on Chaco's northern frontier were collecting huge quantities of wild plants, growing corn, and probably processing large game into dried meat and jerky for export to the central canyon's great houses.

The probability that such late imports made it from the frontier to the general farming population in meaningful quantities is small. Most of the imports were consumed in the canyon's great houses. I base this conclusion on contrasting burial data from Chaco farmsteads and Pueblo Bonito. A baby born in Pueblo Bonito in the mid- to late 1000s was three times more likely to live through childhood than one born in a farmstead less than a mile away. At adulthood, the great-house child was likely to stand one to two inches taller than the farmers' child. In an even more striking contrast, a child born to humble farmers in the Red Mesa Valley after the mid-1000s was only one-fourth as likely to survive to age five as a great-house child at Chaco Canyon.

It was along such differences in quality of life and life possibilities that Chacoan society fractured when it was visited by droughts that peaked in the 1090s and again in the early 1100s. Throughout this period the great-house elites continued to import resources from afar as the producers' plight worsened. New roads, ever more kivas, an emerging class of great-house warriors, and newly walled-off great-house courtyards all announced the economic divisions in ways we fully understand in the industrial world. The elites' centers of production moved to new territory, local producers were further displaced, and class divisions became a deep fracture line weakening the fabric of Chacoan society. The divisions were not unlike those between Wall Street and Main Street in the United States during the banking crisis and economic recession of 2008 to 2010. Regrettably, people around the world today know this scenario of contrasting excess and hardship, of grandiosity and just getting by.

For a time, Chacoan society had cleverly converted traditional hand-tool horticulture in an ungenerous, sometimes capricious, semiarid climate into a political and economic power more impressive than most feudal European princes of the time could have contemplated. But with grandeur came both rigidity and fragility, coupled with staggering, increasingly unmet costs. Chronic problems mounted. For the average farmer, the reward for hard work became more hard work. Even as the last lavish building episodes—to today's tourists, the most visible ones—were taking place at Chaco Canyon, small farmsteads in the outlying districts were being abandoned by the hundreds.

Each abandoned farm further reduced the calories flowing through the immense Chacoan system. Archaeologists familiar with the San Juan Basin have noted that the complex late pottery styles, such as the Chaco-McElmo Black-on-white bowls found at Chetro Ketl, Pueblo Alto, and other great houses in Chaco Canyon, have never been found at most small farmsteads in the central basin. This is unsurprising, for the inhabitants were already gone or were so disconnected from the elites as to have become economically and socially invisible.

As the small farming pueblos were abandoned, new pithouse villages were being built—mostly in higher elevations near the edges of the San Juan Basin. The movement started slowly, then rushed toward a peak at about 1140 to 1150. Ironically, many of the very farmers and villagers needed to sustain Chacoan society had abandoned the Chacoan dream and moved to the higher mesas. By the mid-twelfth century, Chacoan society had ceased to exist. Most of the great houses were abandoned within a generation. The once-huge trade network was bankrupt. It was the end of another chapter for the early Puebloans.

Changing seasons of rainfall, bad crop years, scarce firewood, droughts, disease, malnutrition, and conflict with outsiders have all been advanced as causes for the Chacoan decline. In truth, many things conjoin to bring a great society to its knees, and so it undoubtedly was with Chaco. Exit regional Chacoan society of the western basin lands; enter ancestral Pueblos of the high mesas and cool, upland, ponderosa country of Mesa Verde, the Little Colorado River, and the Rio Grande.

In and around Bandelier National Monument, a new society that would eventually become the Rio Grande Pueblo peoples began during the tumultuous two centuries following Chaco Canyon's decline. The Pajarito Plateau was, I believe, the most important upland crucible in which this new version of ancestral Pueblo society was forged. It also became a primary refuge for that society during new tests to come. Without the Pajarito and the Jemez Mountains as a refuge, quite likely the Rio Grande Pueblo world would not be a growing, contemporary society of more than a dozen native communities. Lessons once learned at Chaco and not repeated on the Pajarito equipped their ancestors for another millennium of survival.

Survival and the Efficiency Lesson

The Upland Period

I n the 1000s they came stealthily, family by family, to the uplands, where they dug deep pithouses tucked away in tiny coves. Later, in the 1100s, as Chacoan society exploded in want and chaos, they came in great rushes as whole villages trekked into the ponderosa-studded canyon lands of the Pajarito Plateau. As people continued to flee the central San Juan Basin in the 1100s, what is now Bandelier National Monument and the northern Rio Grande Valley became a permanent home to the largest surviving remnants of the early Pueblo world.

The period between 1100 and 1300 was one of the most complex in all of Southwestern history. In broad perspective, people moved into the highlands during the 1100s not only in ancestral Pueblo territory but throughout the Southwest. This "upland" period was a time of enormous social and economic upheaval as the Chacoan world fragmented outward in every direction. Archaeologist Stephen Lekson has argued that some Chacoan elites, guided by a cosmological worldview, followed an important meridian north into Colorado's Montezuma Valley while others followed the same meridian south to Casas Grandes, Mexico. Of greater concern to the Pajarito story are the host of ordinary farmers who flooded into the uplands everywhere surrounding the San Juan Basin by the late 1100s.

Some of the places where these emigrants sought refuge were already populated by local highlanders. This appears to have been the case, for example, in the Gallina country on the west face of the Jemez Mountains, which already housed settled villages. Deadly conflicts, presumably between locals and newcomers, raged there for at least half a century. Other areas, such as the Zuni Mountains and the Pajarito Plateau, had relatively few permanent residents, and the process was more peaceful.

Apparently, it was a combination of droughts, food scarcity, and unpredictable social conditions that forced farmers into the higher, wetter mountains as Chaco fell. Evidence for drought, highly unpredictable precipitation, or both in the northern Southwest is clear for the 1080s and 1090s, the early 1100s, and the late 1200s, although conditions varied from

A carbon-painted Santa Fe Black-on-white bowl, the characteristic pottery of the upland period on the Pajarito Plateau. Note the simple design and the "ghostly" quality of the dark gray paint. Photograph by Blair Clark, 1989. Courtesy Museum of New Mexico, catalog number 43341/11.

place to place. The emigrants' dilemma was that although mountainous areas of the Southwest are invariably moister than adjacent lowlands, their shorter growing seasons and cool nighttime temperatures seriously limit crop development. During the 1100s, farmers once well adapted to grow-ing large-cobbed corn in open basins and valleys found themselves crushed into much colder, confined canyons and onto narrow, thin-soiled mesas at sixty-five hundred to seventy-five hundred feet, where their corn grew poorly. The move must also have undone family calculations of how much planted acreage was needed in order to get through the winter. A crucial food efficiency, nearly a thousand years in the making as generations of Chaco-era farmers carefully selected for increasing cob size, was erased in the high country.

Still, the Chacoans and their children, even their children's children, went back to uplands such as Mesa Verde, from which their remote Basketmaker ancestors had descended into the basins during the 700s to 900s, not just to farm but to pursue the mixed horticulture-foraging-hunting economy of their forebears on land some of those forebears had pioneered. Thus, after several centuries of heady power, growth, and experimentation, Chacoans now sought refuge in economic efficiency and family self-sufficiency.

But there was a catch to this impulse to rediscover old traditions. The Basketmaker homelands, such as the Mesa Verde area and the Zuni Mountains, filled up quickly. That left other people to fight their way into the Gallina territory or to avoid confrontation by trickling into the lightly populated and less familiar eastern uplands such as the Pajarito Plateau and the foothills of the Sangre de Cristo Mountains near present-day Taos, New Mexico. These new landscapes had to be learned: soil types varied, patterns of cold updrafts were different, and the climate and ecology of the east faces of the Jemez and Sangre de Cristo Mountains were different from those of the western slopes facing Chaco's old frontier.

Some archaeologists and ethnohistorians believe they have an understanding of this complex era of migrations, derived from studying easily copied architecture and artifacts, especially pottery forms and decorations. But until, or unless, they use the most precise science and follow genetic markers in DNA extracted from human teeth or bones recovered through excavation, their reconstructions of ancient migrations and cultural identities will remain speculative.

We do know that the northern Rio Grande area filled up in the mid-1100s. The evidence can be seen on virtually every south- or east-tilting mesa. It consists of small to medium-size, rough masonry farmsteads, mixed with some pithouses in colder microsettings, and new styles of locally made black-on-white pottery that functionally replaced the Chacoan wares, which had already passed into heirloom status.

In Bandelier National Monument, researchers call these farmsteads "Santa Fe Black-on-white" sites, after the type of pottery most abundant in them. They tend to be found on mesas at middle elevations, those of sixty-five hundred to seventy-two hundred feet. Most of the pueblos consist of six to twelve single-story rooms built of roughly shaped tuff blocks and arranged in a line or in an L shape. Interestingly, many farmsteads lack kivas, suggesting major post-Chaco changes in family religious practices, as has been proposed by archaeologist Lynne Sebastian. The kivas that are found vary significantly in architectural style, inviting questions about the cultural and geographical identities of their creators (again, DNA studies could resolve such questions). These Santa Fe Black-on-white sites were founded primarily from the 1150s into the early 1200s, and their residents pursued a mixed subsistence economy.

The complex relationship between terrain, rainfall, soil type, and temperature has always been critical to understanding climate and agriculture in the Southwest. The Southwest is not all equally dry; an elongated strip of mountainous country stretching from southern Colorado to central New Mexico receives more summer thunderstorms than any other place in the United States. This is due to seasonal air masses and has been a pattern, although an unstable one, since ancient times. After the Chacoan decline, survivors of that world, like some Mogollon people from the declining Mimbres society of southwestern New Mexico, literally moved uphill to unite with the mountain thunders.

But simply getting more moisture to plants wasn't the whole story. Corn is difficult to grow in much of the Southwest. Selecting the right seed corn is even more challenging. In northern uplands such as the Pajarito Plateau, a corn-planting schedule based on the lower-elevation San Juan Basin model would have been disastrous. Researchers can easily underestimate the epic practical problem of relocating a large population into the uplands. That is probably why many of the Santa Fe Black-on-white farmsteads of the Pajarito were situated in the middle elevations. This would have maximized the growing season, moderated cold nighttime temperatures, and allowed at least some corn to be grown. But what was everyone else to do after those prized settings were claimed? Experimentation with different elevations offered one answer. At the end of the upland period, scattering to new locales provided another.

The practical implications of living at one elevation or another are still with us today. Albuquerque, at fifty-one hundred feet above sea level, receives an average of only eight to ten inches of rainfall per year. Santa Fe, at seven thousand feet in a basin of the Sangre de Cristo Mountains, receives an average of thirteen inches. Los Alamos, at seventy-two hundred feet on the wetter, east-facing Pajarito, receives almost twenty inches per year. More abundant moisture notwithstanding, any resident of Los Alamos can tell you how difficult it is to raise a crop of tall, large-cobbed corn in a backyard garden. Cool nighttime temperatures and a short growing season are the culprits. The same variety of corn will generally produce successively smaller ears from Albuquerque to Santa Fe to Los Alamos.

It was much the same in ancient times. Corncobs excavated from ruins of the 1100s in the higher elevations around Bandelier Monument are small in comparison with cobs found in earlier Chacoan sites of the San Juan Basin. Archaeologists have long been puzzled by this upland corn, pronouncing it "retrogressive," "stunted," and "primitive." Some such corn might have been throwback varieties, because local crossbreeding quickly introduces unexpected genetic variation in corn. Other varieties were probably lost as hungry Chacoan farmers ate their seed corn in desperation. But much of the corn uncovered in ancient caches and ruins in and around Bandelier was probably disappointingly small because of stunting by cool nighttime temperatures. Perhaps it should be no surprise that the large variety now known as "Pueblo corn," likely newly hybridized, did not appear in quantity until three centuries later at the huge Classic period pueblos along the Rio Grande.

The genetics of prehistoric corn, rather than its appearance, is information still largely unavailable to Southwestern anthropologists. It was even less available, of course, to native peoples. Archaeologist Linda Cordell recently pointed out that the ancients who carefully selected seed corn to produce blue-kerneled cobs could have been choosing from among any number of genetic variants. That is, the outward appearance of corn has surprisingly little to do with its inner genetics. Ancient farmers selecting seed corn on the basis of outward appearances were, rather like roulette players in Las Vegas, betting on fate as much as anything. That would have made the specific field source and purity of seed corn critical information. But people traded over considerable distances during seasons of want; did the end receivers even know the corn's source? Would a bowlful of seeds still be pure and unmixed? Anthropologists and archaeologists cannot currently answer these questions. All seed corn was not equally valuable, but farmers could not be sure they were getting exactly what they wanted just by looking at it.

In response to such conundrums, humans have often sought answers in faith, ritual, and religion. The Chacoans seem to have entwined rituals, storerooms, and corn into an impressive driving force, but that formula failed when tested against the reality of the uplands. Even the Chaco elites who moved north to the Montezuma Valley of Colorado in the 1100s would have experienced the failure of their rules for accurately selecting corn for planting at their higher-elevation great houses. Perhaps disillusionment with rituals that proved ineffective, first during the Chacoan droughts of the early 1100s and again in the uplands, explains the dearth of Chaco-style kivas in the Pajarito farmsteads of the late 1100s.

The substantial mass of population that had characterized the Chacoan system simply could not be immediately supported on the reduced crop yields imposed by the highlands. Hunting and foraging again became equally or even more important than farming. But hunting and foraging require a great deal of space and support only low population densities. Some people starved; others raided in the Gallina country. Violence and homicide became epic in the high country adjoining Chaco's eastern frontier in the mid- to late 1100s. Considering the large population and the ecological limitations of farming in the mountains, it should be no surprise that the twelfth century was exceedingly difficult.

Before the late 1000s, the Chacoan trade network had softened the hard edge of local scarcity over thousands of square miles. More than a dozen varieties of elaborate, painted pottery were regularly traded between hundreds of well-built villages. The labor invested in creating prized pottery could buy corn, and district granaries could at least provide secure supplies of seed corn in poor years. But the Chacoan economic network had already disintegrated before present-day Bandelier Monument began to fill up. This pushed even more impoverished families of common farmers high into the Pajarito Plateau, and locally made pottery was supplemented only occasionally by one or two trade vessels. Consequently, Pajarito sites of the 1100s rarely have much fine tradeware pottery.

When archaeologists first began to understand the Chaco phenomenon, many of them found it difficult to believe that after the Chaco decline, progress and evolution in architectural styles "ran backward," in that pithouses reappeared after more than two centuries of above-ground pueblo architecture in western New Mexico. But this development should not be so surprising; nearly eight hundred years later, Anglo-American homesteaders in Texas, Oklahoma, and eastern New Mexico built sod-roofed dugouts to live in until their first few crops were harvested. Only later did such "sodbusters" build the neat frame houses and churches considered typical of the Midwestern, Euro-American society from which most of them came.

The first post-Chaco settlements of deep pithouses were generally hidden away in mountainous areas across the Four Corners country. Some archaeologists find such sites frustrating because, like the niche separation of the 800s, when Basketmaker, Pueblo I, and Pueblo II settlements were coeval in the Gallup district, they ruin the tidy, normative descriptors and neat developmental charts found in textbooks. The upland pithouses are often characterized as "isolated kivas" or as "atypical," "misdated," or "contaminated" by pottery made long after the pithouse itself was dug. But the settlements are there, nonetheless—scant testimony to several generations who made a difficult adaptation to life in the uplands. On the Pajarito Plateau, immigrant farmers made out as best they could, without the benefits of Chacoan economic and political power or, judging from the scarcity of kivas, large religious structures.

Within a generation, by 1150 to 1190, styles of architecture on the Pajarito Plateau had become more "normal," and small, masonry, Santa Fe Black-on-white pueblos were being built in the more moderate elevations of the piñon-juniper zone. New forms of black-on-white pottery, including Santa Fe Black-on-white itself, characterize this period throughout the northern uplands. Instead of crushing iron ore to create black pigments, as was done for the earlier Chacoan vessels, potters began to use plant (carbon-based) pigments to create bold black-on-white designs.

For most archaeologists, the appearance of carbon-paint pottery in above-ground masonry pueblos of six to thirty-six rooms marks the real beginning of what they call the Coalition period in the northern Rio Grande, which dates from about 1150 or 1170 to 1290 CE. The organic paint technique is usually described as having moved from the Kayenta area of northern Arizona to the Mesa Verde country and thence to the Rio Grande. I favor the Kayenta explanation because connections with Arizona—both the ancestral Pueblo and Hohokam districts—might have created important conduits for knowledge about how to farm corn in the pumice fields and rocky mesa terrains of the Pajarito Plateau. But many archaeologists believe it is more accurate to associate the rise of carbon-paint pottery manufacture in the highlands of the Southwest with the simultaneous decline of Chacoan society in the lower elevations.

In Bandelier, the most easily identified carbon-paint pottery of the upland period is Santa Fe Black-on-white. This pottery was decorated with bold but ghostly, off-black designs over a light gray background. Hundreds of small masonry pueblos built on the Pajarito Plateau during the late 1100s contain this pottery, but few of them have been excavated. These sites have generated only sporadic interest among archaeologists or

The Chaco Canyon ruins called Chetro Ketl (foreground) and "the Annex." Chetro
Ketl illustrates the planned, rectilinear form common to many of the later great houses.
© Baker Aerial Archaeology—Tom Baker, negative 60038.

Aerial view of the network of ancient roads that joined near Pueblo Alto, on the mesa behind (north of) and above Pueblo Bonito. The roads appear in the photograph as five relatively straight lines running from the foreground to converge at the apex of a rough triangle in the center distance. © Baker Aerial Archaeology—Tom Baker, negative 74398.

View looking west down the Chaco River toward Pueblo Bonito (at center right). Most of Chaco Canyon's great houses backed up to the dramatic sandstone mesa on the right, facing south. © Baker Aerial Archaeology—Tom Baker, negative 60045.

Aerial view of Frijoles Canyon in midwinter. Notice the sunlit, south-facing side of the canyon in contrast to its snowy north face (left). Tyuonyi and Bandelier Monument Headquarters in lower center. © Baker Aerial Archaeology—Tom Baker, negative 44629.

Summer scene of Tyuonyi (foreground) and Talus House, Frijoles Canyon.
© Baker Aerial Archaeology—Tom Baker.

Aerial view over the mesa that housed the large, riverine period pueblo of Tsankawi. The outline of the ruins can be seen at the center of the photograph. © Baker Aerial Archaeology—Tom Baker, negative 45289.

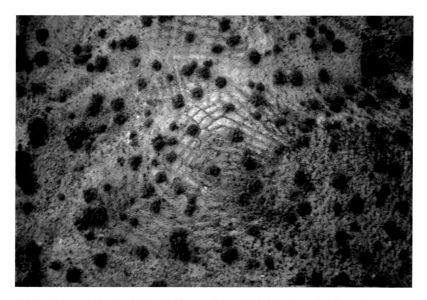

Grid gardens near Tsankawi. These hilltop gardens, gridded by lines of cobbles to slow run-off and retain moisture, illustrate the dramatic engineering of the landscape that typified the 1200s to 1500s in the northern Rio Grande. © Baker Aerial Archaeology—Tom Baker.

Talus House, 2004. This pueblo was reconstructed by archaeologists using a crew of San Ildefonso Pueblo stonemasons in the 1930s. Courtesy National Park Service, Bandelier National Monument.

Aerial view of the cliff-top pueblo of Puye, to the north of Bandelier National Monument. Puye typifies the sites of the riverine, or Classic, period that were reestablished on the Pajarito Plateau when droughts were severe. © Baker Aerial Archaeology—Tom Baker, negative 46955.

A grooved stone axe from the Pajarito Plateau, once hafted to a wood handle for felling small trees. Courtesy National Park Service, Bandelier National Monument.

Aerial view of Pueblo Colorado, in the Galisteo Basin southeast of Santa Fe, New Mexico. This site is typical of riverine period villages in the Rio Grande Valley at lower elevations than the Pajarito Plateau. © Baker Aerial Archaeology—Tom Baker, negative 72301.

(Above): A San Clemente Glaze A Polychrome bowl dating to the early Riverine period, or the 1300s. Courtesy Michael P. Marshall, Maxwell Museum Collections. (Right): A Sankawe Black-on-cream jar, a distinctive style produced on the Pajarito Plateau during the late riverine period, from 1500 to 1650. Courtesy Michael P. Marshall, Maxwell Museum Collections.

Fig. 14. Site LA-4632 at completion of excavation.

Plan of site LA 4632, a typical, twenty-room, Santa Fe Black-on-white pueblo of the late 1100s to early 1200s. Hallmarks of these small pueblos are fairly evenly sized rooms built of volcanic tuff blocks, few kivas, and only modest evidence of renovations or redesign. Note the slightly larger communal room in the right (east) center of the site. Courtesy Bandelier National Monument and Los Alamos National Laboratory.

the public, because they are neither visually spectacular nor rich in cultural material. Most were inhabited for only a generation or two, so they yield few museum specimens and little accurately datable material. Ironically, they and the rarer pithouses dug on the Pajarito north of Bandelier Monument, which date between the late 1000s and 1155 CE, could hold the important clues to the adaptations made by the first generation or two of post-Chaco immigrants.

Indeed, data from excavations at major ruins and from archaeological surveys often yield different pictures of what happened in ancient times; it is unsafe to re-create the past on the basis of only one or the other. Nearly all the Pajarito's several dozen large, partially excavated sites were founded after the late 1200s, but an intensive archaeological survey conducted on adjacent land between 1977 and 1980 turned up another 880 sites. About 55 percent of these dated to the Coalition period (1150–1290), whereas just under 30 percent belonged to the Rio Grande Classic period (1325–1600). Yet virtually all the literature written about Bandelier National Monument until that time covered the Classic period. Some researchers even portray Bandelier as having been inhabited only between 1300 and 1600, although the most extensive habitation in the monument actually spanned the years from about 1175 to 1290. The sequence was then interrupted for several generations, until monument land again became heavily populated when Puebloans who had moved down along the Rio Grande in the late 1200s began using it for alternative, upland farms during dry years in the 1300s. A second, impressive population peak apparently came during a time of intense droughts in the 1400s, even though late Pueblo society remained firmly rooted in the lower, riverine elevations.

Certainly, the Pajarito Plateau was more heavily used than some other parts of the Southwest during the upland period. An analysis of archaeological projects conducted throughout the Chaco country between 1960 and 1985 indicates an average of just over twelve sites per square mile in large areas over which archaeological teams on foot looked painstakingly at every square yard. A survey of land adjacent to Bandelier, however, conducted by archaeologists from the University of California, Los Angeles in the mid-1980s, found that about twenty ancient sites per square mile were built on the Pajarito, nearly double the Chaco average.

A survey conducted some years ago by the National Park Service in Bandelier itself charted 470 new archaeological sites in only 3,356 acres of mesa land adjacent to the middle elevations of Frijoles Canyon. The majority of them dated to the upland period and averaged to a staggering ninety sites per square mile at that time. This density of sites probably reflects farmers' preference for the slightly longer growing season and greater foraging productivity at that elevation than at higher ones. Only the greatest Chacoan outliers of a century earlier, with their nearby farmsteads, and a few late Rio Grande Classic pueblos show similar intensity of land use anywhere in the eastern Puebloan world. And in the Chaco country, that high site density prevailed over only a few square miles surrounding the largest, oldest great houses.

The high figure for site density in Frijoles Canyon itself did not hold up during the large surveys of other, more rugged parts of Bandelier carried out in the late 1990s or the ones that monument archaeologist Rory Gauthier is still pursuing. This is not unexpected, because Frijoles Creek carries twice as many acre-feet of water per year as any other stream in Bandelier Monument and so was more desirable to farmers. (Several canyons north of the monument boundary carry more water than Frijoles Creek and, correspondingly, have higher site densities and larger sites.) Archaeological sites in the Southwest are not scattered randomly across the landscape; they cluster densely in places of good soils, surface water, and transitions between environmental zones.

By roughly 1225, the majority of the small Santa Fe Black-on-white pueblos on the Pajarito Plateau had been built. These sites are most numerous north of the monument, near well-watered canyons such as those called Guaje and Bayo. One example in the monument itself is "House Across the Way," near the mouth of Alamo Canyon at an elevation of only fifty-four hundred feet—a bit lower than most other sites of its time. This eight-room pueblo had more kinds of pottery than the earliest Santa Fe Black-on-white sites, but most of its undecorated, gray-to-buff cooking pots were still made locally. Exotic trade goods such as semiprecious stones, shells, and feathers are seldom found in Pajarito sites of this time period.

In the early 1200s, the Pajarito's ancestral clans began to build what Euro-Americans later romanticized with the name "cliff palaces." These villages indicate a general shift to higher elevations, seven thousand to seventy-five hundred feet, that characterized most of the 1200s and is not yet fully explained. Although tree-ring dates of 1300 to 1400 are generally given for the Pajarito cliff ruins, such as Long House and Talus House in Frijoles Canyon, the wood that produced those dates was retrieved as fragments of beams that early-twentieth-century archaeologists discarded in the dirt they removed when they dug the ruins. Exactly where in the excavated sites those timbers were originally placed is usually in doubt. In addition, many of the structures were remodeled and repaired repeatedly, and beams used in the renovations have relatively late dates. As a consequence, few sites near the Bandelier visitor center have been dated with satisfactory precision.

Throughout the Southwest, however, the major construction at most of the larger cliff dwellings took place from roughly 1200 or 1220 to 1275, and the oldest pottery found on the eroding talus slopes below Long House and Talus House at Bandelier dates generally to this period. In the mid-1200s, even as the cliff houses expanded, yet another wave of immigrants may have filtered onto the southern Pajarito Plateau from other upland areas, according to a number of experts. Their pueblos often had one or two kivas, some of which show Mesa Verdean configurations. The architecture of the Pajarito became more diverse at this time.

The ancient cliff houses of the Southwest were both utilitarian and magnificent to behold. They generally sat in good defensive locations where they were difficult to attack. The large, community kivas and granary towers built into many of the cliff houses suggests that they served as wintering places for farmers who spent the summers in their farmsteads. Energy efficient, they acted as huge solar collectors to absorb the sun's winter rays; virtually every Southwestern cliff dwelling faces south, southeast, or southwest. Yet most of them were cool in summer because they were protected from the high-angle summer sun by rock overhangs. On the Pajarito Plateau, local geology made the cliff-side settings somewhat less protected from the summer sun than elsewhere, so cave rooms compensated. But even on the Pajarito, the cliff-side architecture accurately captures the efficiency theme of the entire upland period.

At Bandelier, every one of the fascinating cliff dwellings with cave rooms, including Long House and Talus House, is found on the north side of Frijoles Creek, facing south. In winter, while the sunlit entrances of snow-free rooms line the north wall of the canyon, deep snow often lingers for weeks on the canyon's opposite cliff face, looking north. Ambient temperatures on those two canyon faces differ by as much as twenty degrees Fahrenheit on a December day. Sharp-eyed visitors will notice that as they pass along the current cliff trail, the number and sizes of the ancient rooms diminish dramatically when the trail ducks behind a rock pinnacle that shades part of the cliff face. Winter warmth meant not only greater comfort but also substantially less need for firewood to heat residential rooms.

Cave rooms that once formed part of a cliff dwelling below Otowi Ruin on the Pajarito Plateau. The cliff faces south. Courtesy Museum of New Mexico, negative number 41997.

Some higher, isolated cave rooms fashioned during both the upland and the later Rio Grande Classic periods sit above Frijoles Canyon and near Otowi Ruin and Puye Cliffs, on the Pajarito Plateau to the north of the monument. These likely served as winter retreats for Pajarito families, because the soft tuff of the plateau supplied too few good, south-facing cliffs with stable rock overhangs to shelter every outlying pueblo. The cave rooms compensated, again raising the possibility that the plateau's thin, mesa-top soil cover and easily worked tuff made cave rooms a natural replacement for the deep pithouses and winter kivas or community houses of other places such as Mesa Verde, where sandstone dominated.

Cliff houses and cave rooms were not sited haphazardly, for many mountain canyons in the Southwest are subject to brutal "wind tunnel" effects during winter storms and at times when cold evening winds rush through them. Tijeras Canyon, through which Interstate 25 passes east of Albuquerque, is one locally well-known wind tunnel. No ancient dwellings at all are found against the most exposed portions of its rugged, south-facing wall. People undoubtedly avoided some canyons on the Pajarito because of similar microclimatic quirks.

But however efficiently heated the cliff houses were, they did not become the primary form of architecture on the Pajarito during the upland centuries. Within a few hundred yards to several miles of most of the major cliff dwellings, there are usually dozens or more contemporaneous, ordinary farmstead pueblos. Many of these can be found on the district's flat mesa tops, above cave rooms. Some are strung out along the upper reaches of one or another of the canyons that crosscut the plateau, and still others were built in the canyon bottoms.

Complicating most architecture-based archaeological chronologies, yet another wave of deep pithouse construction took place in much of the upland Southwest (though not on the southern Pajarito) that was coeval with the cliff dwellings. These pithouses are found throughout the Southwest at elevations of sixty-three hundred to roughly seventy-three hundred feet. Judging from a number of excavated ones, they have a mean date of 1223 CE. Because the upland pithouses are deeper than expected for their elevation, I am tempted to assume that the extra thermal buffering of a deep pithouse means the climate was much colder at this time. This idea correlates nicely with the boom in south-facing cliff houses and expansion in the number of cave rooms at Bandelier. It also suggests significant climate change—a serious complication for upland farmers. More complications followed. Droughts came in the later 1200s, and some people probably shifted to farming lower canyon floors, even as others built large, mesa-top pueblos at higher elevations than the existing cliff houses. In short, the upland period became a time in which no single solution prevailed. As a consequence, most archaeological texts focus on the large, architecturally interesting pueblos of the late 1200s—the consummation, in most interpretive schemes, of the Coalition period—and gloss over the other developments of the 1270s to early 1300s.

But the subplots of adaptation to social and environmental forces during periods of great uncertainty beg to be considered. One clue to ponder is the reappearance of multiple, coeval architectural styles in slightly different ecological niches in the same general locale. That pattern was the signature of rapid change in the Gallup area of the 800s CE, and I believe it was the signature of change in the upland period, too.

Understanding the Upland Period

People's general shift in the mid- to late 1200s to living at the higher elevations of the Pajarito Plateau, with their short growing seasons, is difficult to reconcile with the desirability of raising relatively large-cobbed corn. Might it be that although the larger sites on the plateau now sat at somewhat higher elevations than the cliff houses, their residents actually shifted many of their corn plots downhill to the canyon floors?

The cliff house granaries of the early to mid-1200s throughout the Southwest indicate that harvests from the mesa tops above them were carried downhill when farmers consolidated in the cliff villages to share and protect their crops over the winter. In contrast, it seems plausible that during the drought-ridden late 1200s, people grew their corn along canyon-bottom watercourses and then carried the harvested ears uphill for the winter, in order not to lose their investment in the infrastructure of cliff dwellings and newer mesa-top sites. Moreover, canyon-bottom farmsteads might easily have been raided in the late 1200s as part of drought-induced conflict. Was that why people built Tyuonyi in Frijoles Canyon in the 1280s or 1290s? This large, fortified, streamside pueblo would have made great sense if scattered canyon-bottom farmers consolidated there to reduce their vulnerability. Perhaps their consolidation impelled the proliferation of "field houses"—small structures where people lived temporarily while tending distant fields—which appear all along Bandelier's canyons at this time. These issues merit further investigation, and Bandelier holds the archaeological inventory necessary to resolve the question.

At national monuments, emphasis is placed on preservation, so relatively little excavation has been done using modern scientific methods in Bandelier itself. The great period of excavation in the monument came before World War II. Indeed, in Frijoles Canyon, most excavations at the largest sites were completed even before World War I. Now there are several modern excavation reports to consult for medium-size sites in the monument area. Several other extensive excavation reports from the early 1980s are available for the mesas north of Bandelier and for the lower canyon mouths

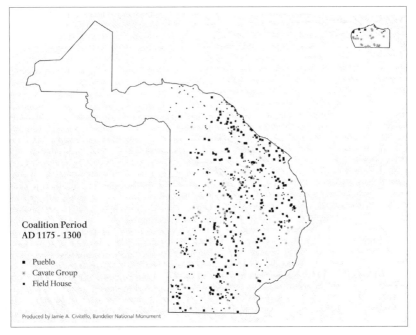

Archaeological sites of the upland (Coalition) period in Bandelier National Monument, 1175–1300. Note the profusion of field houses dotting the landscape around the pueblos. Courtesy Jamie Civitello and Bandelier National Monument.

near, or now in, Cochiti Reservoir. These are invaluable, but the archaeology of the lower elevations along the Rio Grande is somewhat different from that of Bandelier's piñon and ponderosa zones, which look down on the river country.

Using survey results, modest test excavations, and reports from lower elevations along the Rio Grande, archaeologists have pieced together a general picture of the thirteenth century in the Bandelier area. Some unusually severe winters may have struck the northern Rio Grande in the early 1200s, for along with cliff houses, the thermally efficient pithouses mentioned earlier were again being built. Examples have been found near Taos, in the Gallina area, in central New Mexico, and farther south, in the Sierra Blanca. As with the highland pithouses of a century earlier, many archaeologists still reserve judgment on just what these can tell us until more are found, excavated, and dated by laboratory methods. Yet these later pithouses share some striking characteristics: they are found primarily in moderate (and therefore relatively warm) elevations of about sixty-five hundred feet; they average between two and two and a half feet deep; and unlike the Southwest's upland pithouses of the mid-1100s, they often contain surprising quantities of well-made trade pottery. They are not kivas. Unexcavated, they look from the ground surface no different from kivas, but when excavated, they typically have ordinary hearths and household artifacts without any of the special architectural features unique to the true sacred chambers.

The most common trade pottery found in these small pithouse settlements (and in some of the Pajarito's Santa Fe Black-on-white sites) is St. Johns Polychrome (black and white over red) and its variants, which usually make up about 2 percent of all the pottery at a site. This pottery, traded into mountainous areas near Albuquerque, Bandelier, and Mesa Verde, was manufactured in the uplands of east-central Arizona near the town of St. Johns, as well as in the Zuni area, about 150–200 miles southwest of Bandelier Monument. The presence of trade wares from distant, western localities is significant, for it tells us that a highland trading network had replaced the old Chacoan trading patterns after more than a half-century's interruption. Distant trading partners were being selected from the upland piñon-ponderosa districts of eastern Arizona, where agriculture had already been practiced for centuries in cinder fields and other forms of volcanic soils, which were similar to the Pajarito's.

Trade undoubtedly brought seed corn, pigments, and exotics to the Pajarito Plateau. It also created a critical flow of knowledge that might have sped up people's adaptation to the Pajarito's distinctly non-Chacoan geology and ecology. With that knowledge conduit, change accelerated on the plateau, the Coalition period moved into high gear, and kivas returned as a standard part of the architectural repertoire. Large percentages of St. Johns Polychrome pottery found in surface surveys throughout the Southwestern uplands can be used to measure the size, shape, and ecological dimensions of a post-Chacoan renaissance in the mid-1200s.

Just after 1200 in the Bandelier area, cliff houses, small pueblos with kivas, and cave rooms could all be found within a few miles of one another. Each architectural style is found in a slightly different setting. In other areas, pithouses also formed part of the mix. In Bandelier itself, many of the early, smaller, Santa Fe Black-on-white pueblos were soon abandoned. A bit later, new pueblos were being established a thousand feet lower, near Cochiti Reservoir. One example, Kiva House, never reoccupied during the Rio Grande Classic period (after 1300), consisted of twenty-one rooms and

St. Johns Polychrome bowl, about 1175 to 1275. This type of pottery was a widely traded hallmark of the later upland period. Courtesy Michael P. Marshall, Maxwell Museum Collections.

three kivas, and its residents used a dozen styles of painted pottery. Unlike most of the small Santa Fe Black-on-white sites of the Pajarito mesas, it was renovated for reuse in the late 1200s.

A similar and more famous site, Pindi Pueblo, just west of modern Santa Fe along the Santa Fe River, was founded at this time. Immortalized as "LA 1," Pindi Pueblo was the first site assigned a number by the Laboratory of Anthropology, a Santa Fe research institution now part of the Museum of New Mexico, which maintains records on more than 180,000 archaeological sites. Kiva House, Pindi Pueblo, and a village called Colina Verde in the Galisteo Basin, southeast of Santa Fe, are proof that at about 1200 to 1250 the Pueblo world had begun tentatively to look downhill again from its remote mountaintops. But most of these lowland settlements, possibly established to recapture a longer growing season during a time of colder temperatures, were fairly quickly abandoned, and the early Puebloans did not rebuild them until a century or so later. Meanwhile, the highland settlements continued to flourish.

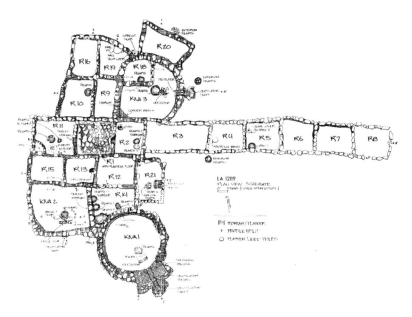

Plan of Kiva House (LA 12119). Sites such as this, built a bit later than the Santa Fe Black-on-white farmsteads, have kivas that often vary in architectural detail, indicating immigration from other upland areas in the mid- to late 1200s. Courtesy Bandelier National Monument.

By the late 1200s, huge, mesa-top pueblos with plazas were being built throughout the Pajarito Plateau and on similar mesas from eastern Arizona north into Colorado—although by Chacoan standards, they were still few and far-flung. It turns out that the northern Rio Grande's Coalition period patterns were being experienced over at least a hundred thousand square miles.

Most of the large, mesa-top Pajarito villages consist of fallen tiers of rooms built of rough, rectangular blocks hand-carved from the Pajarito's relatively soft volcanic tuff. A textbook example of such a site is LA 12700, also known as Guaje Canyon Ruin, which lies about one and a half miles north of Los Alamos. It straddles a narrow, sloping mesa top on U.S. Forest Service land, at about seven thousand feet above sea level. Each of its three immense, rectangular room blocks encloses a plaza. Remarkably, this plaza site also contains five deep, circular kivas, carefully hand-pecked into the soft bedrock. Guaje Canyon Ruin and the Bandelier Monument sites of Burnt Mesa Pueblo, Alamo Mesa, and several similar sites represent a late chapter in the Pajarito's upland period.

Villages such as Guaje Canyon Ruin seem to have been built in the late 1200s, only to be abandoned within twenty or thirty years. Some were renovated later, during the Classic period. Like the Guaje site, a number of others scattered across the uplands of northwestern New Mexico have reservoirs built nearby. Such reservoirs are one signature of the mesa-top sites of the mid- to late 1200s. The reservoirs would have greatly reduced the labor needed to haul water up to a pueblo (that is, they were efficient) and would have significantly increased self-sufficiency in the event of a siege or attack.

These multiple styles of architecture and shifting community settings are only part of the story, because agricultural fields also shifted repeatedly. High-elevation pumice fields—unknown and unavailable to Chacoan ancestors—were farmed intensively in the 1200s, although few of them have adjacent large pueblos, probably because only a few corn crops were possible before soil nutrients were exhausted. (In the Southwest, the natural cycle of soil replenishment can take twenty years or more.) On the lower mesa tops, some areas were neatly gridded off into small garden plots. Cobble-mulched gardens first became widespread in the later 1200s, probably as another response to drying conditions. These cobble beds appear at first to be unlikely gardens, but they actually create good conditions for planting in areas where natural evaporation rates are high, as they are in the high, dry, sunny Four Corners country. Cobble- or gravel-mulched garden plots had already long been used in the Tucson basin and south into Sonora, Mexico, before appearing in the Four Corners country and the northern Rio Grande.

Each spring, for hundreds of years, some farmers on the Pajarito must have had to hand-carry water to young plants. During the late spring, when seeds must germinate and when tender young plants can be hopelessly scorched on a single bright, dry, windy afternoon, every drop of moisture retained in the soil is critical. In the area around Bandelier, dark, angular basalt rocks were sometimes used to mulch the rocky grid gardens. Other mulches consisted of dun-colored gravels. Moisture was trapped on the cool underside of the rock, where it touched the soil. Underneath, the earth remained much cooler and moister than the thin, unmodified, mesa-top soil just a few feet away. Cobble beds not only retarded the drying out of the soil but also released sun-captured heat at night to effectively lengthen the growing season and create a more salutary, frost-free micro-environment in which to grow somewhat larger-cobbed corn. Late upland

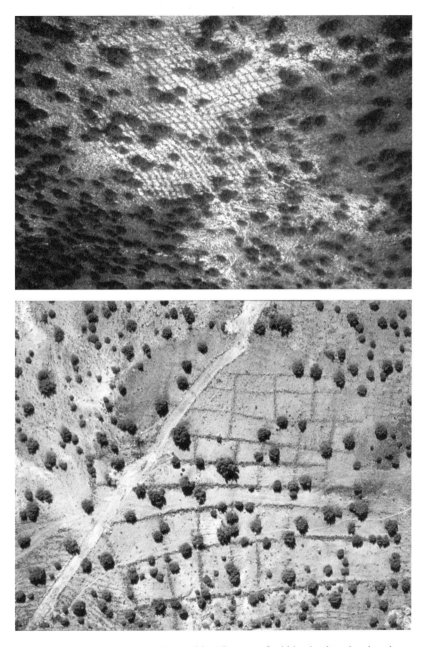

Grid gardens near contemporary Zia Pueblo. The rows of cobbles dividing the plots slow runoff, and finer gravel in the grid floors helps the soil retain moisture. Such gardens were an efficient innovation characteristic of the upland period on the Pajarito Plateau and elsewhere. Top photo shows gardens in flat terrain; bottom shows canyon bottom gardens. © Baker Aerial Archaeology—Tom Baker.

corn did generally increase in size, but we do not know whether this was the result of genetic changes in corn; a period of warmer, wetter weather; or innovative gardening techniques.

The insulation of natural volcanic pumice fields is, if anything, even more effective than that of cobbles and gravel. Porous pumice pebbles also absorb moisture, which is later released as it is heated by the sun. Once wetted, the pumice becomes even more insulating. The moisture to wet the pumice often came from late spring snowmelt in Bandelier's higher elevations. The pumice itself retarded the melt even more, creating a late moistening process that gave upland farmers one more tiny germination advantage during unusually dry springs. Such springs came often in the late 1200s, but each nutrient-poor pumice field was only a short-term, field-diversifying solution. Instead, it was the highly efficient, human-engineered cobble or gravel mulching in the piñon-juniper zone that became the mainstay of sustainable upland agriculture. Investment in such infrastructure, as in the carefully terraced rice paddies of traditional Indonesia, is one hallmark of efficient societies.

Other efficient technological innovations came to Bandelier during the upland period. Among them were axes of very dense stone that were fully grooved for better hafting, improvements that made them far more effective for cutting firewood than earlier, less securely hafted axes of softer stone. The new axes were used to roughly chop roof beams, which later were often trimmed to length by fire. Another example is full-slab sandstone metates, whose large grinding surfaces speeded up the production of cornmeal.

Plaza sites of the late 1200s were once thought to lie mainly north of Bandelier and to have been built by ancestors of today's Tewa-speaking Pueblo Indians—those who come from the pueblos of Ohkay Owinge (formerly San Juan), Santa Clara, San Ildefonso, Nambe, and Tesuque. Sites in Frijoles Canyon and to the south were thought to have been built by ancestors of the eastern Keres-speaking Pueblos—those from Cochiti, Kewa (formerly Santo Domingo), San Felipe, Santa Ana, and Zia. But cultural identity was not the sole factor. Recent field investigations and analyses of aerial photographs indicate that the largest plaza sites actually tend to be situated on mesas where rainfall was comparatively abundant and where small streams flowed in the canyons below. In other words, local ecology appears to have played a large role in their residents' decisions about where to build. It happens that there are simply more well-watered canyons north of Bandelier than to the south. Higher rates of water flow and levels of soil

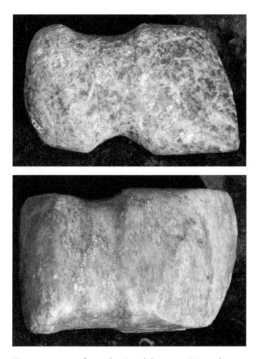

Two stone axes from the Bandelier area. Note the grooves encircling the ax heads, which enabled their users to tie them securely to a wood handle. Courtesy National Park Service, Bandelier National Monument.

A slab metate (center) and other cooking implements typical of the late upland period. The grinding surface of the metate is even larger than those of earlier, Chacoan times. Courtesy National Park Service, Bandelier National Monument.

nutrients probably account more for these larger sites than do the inferred cultural habits of ancestral Tewas as opposed to ancestral Keres people. Thus, the study of local pottery styles (rather than site size) during the 1200s becomes extraordinarily important in helping to sort out who, culturally, was who, as explained in the accompanying piece by archaeologist Rory Gauthier.

Pottery Styles and Cultural Identity in the Northern Rio Grande, 1150–1550

R. P. Gauthier

Early in the upland period, the first locally made pottery was a mineral-paint-decorated ware that resembled ceramic types from the Chaco area. This pottery type, which archaeologists call Kwahe Black-on-white, is widely distributed throughout the northern Rio Grande, reaching as far north as Taos and the Rio Chama area and southward into the vicinity of Santa Fe. The type is found in small quantities in early pueblo sites in Bandelier National Monument.

Slightly later, a new style appeared that was also related to late Chacoan styles. It resembles Chaco-McElmo Black-on-white and is possibly also related to Mesa Verde Black-on-white pottery. The new style is called Santa Fe Black-on-white, and it was the first carbon-paint-decorated ware to be made in the Rio Grande region. It was a major departure from the earlier Chacoan types and the locally made Kwahe Black-on-white, with its mineral paint decorations. The shift from mineral paint to carbon paint is believed to have taken place first in the Kayenta area of northeastern Arizona or possibly farther east, in the Mesa Verde–San Juan area. Whatever the source, around 1175 the carbon-painted Santa Fe Black-on-white was the most common pottery type found in the northern Rio Grande.

Archaeologists generally believe that the wide distribution and similarities of ceramic styles found to the west reflect the migration of populations from the Chaco and Mesa Verde areas to the northern Rio Grande. The wide, upland distribution of Santa Fe Black-on-white also suggests that this kind of pottery was used by many ethnic groups. It is found in the Taos district, which was home to Tiwa speakers; in the Tewa homeland along the Rio Chama, around Santa Fe, and on the Pajarito Plateau; in the Bandelier and Cochiti areas of the Keres language group; and to the immediate west in the Towa-speaking Jemez district.

Only in the early riverine, or Classic, period did ceramic styles begin to correlate notably with ethnic or language groupings, although there were some exceptions. Beginning around 1300 or 1325, glaze-decorated pottery appeared in the area south of Albuquerque and was quickly adopted throughout the Keres area and in the Galisteo Basin, where speakers of both Keres and the now-extinct Tano language lived. In contrast, glaze-decorated pottery was uncommon in the Tewa area, north of Frijoles Canyon. It was also rare in the Jemez area, where a style called Jemez Black-on-white—a carbon-paint-decorated type derived from Santa Fe Black-on-white—was used continuously from 1300 to historic times.

Jemez Black-on-white bowl.
Courtesy Michael P. Marshall,
Maxwell Museum Collections.

North of Frijoles Canyon, in the Tewa areas of the northern Pajarito Plateau and the Rio Chama, a succession of carbon-painted wares appeared, starting with a style that resembled Santa Fe Black-on-white but was made with a different clay source. This type is referred to as Wiyo Black-on-white. It was followed by a succession of styles that all have carbon-paint decorations: Abiquiu Black-on-gray, Bandelier Black-on-gray, and Sankawi Black-on-cream.

The archaeological sites in Frijoles Canyon are generally accepted as ancestral Keres, with an emphasis on the fact that this was the homeland of the people of Cochiti. To the north of Frijoles is the Tewa homeland, specifically the sites of Tsirege, Navawi, Tsankawi, and Otowi. Otowi was the progenitor of San Ildefonso Pueblo. The ceramic styles found at these sites reflect the difference: from Frijoles Canyon south to present-day Cochiti, glaze-decorated pottery predominates, whereas to the north, carbon-decorated pottery of the Tewa groups is the dominant style.

Overall, the mid- to late 1200s saw the resurgence of larger-cobbed corn, important innovations in agriculture, a large-village society, and a well-defined trade network over great sectors of the highland Southwest. The trade network spread production and resource risks among many distant pockets of upland settlements pursuing mixed economies. This strategy somewhat mitigated the Southwest's patchy rainfall by tying highlands together over an east-west distance of 200 to 225 miles, from Taos to eastern Arizona. North-south trade connections connected northerly areas with frigid winters, such as the Taos and Chama valleys, with warmer, southerly ones such as the middle Rio Grande and the chain of mesas that form the northern approach to the Plains of San Augustin. But this far-flung trade network, which can be identified by St. Johns Polychrome pottery and its variants, did not equally incorporate the intervening lowland districts.

Large villages of this period were situated primarily on easily defended mesas, with garden plots both adjacent to the villages and in the canyon bottoms below. Such sites exhibit several styles of horticulture, and those with reservoirs could withstand extended sieges. Even though some larger-cobbed corn was again being grown, foraging remained important. On the Pajarito, the largest plaza sites contain more than four hundred ground-floor rooms, more than some of the fabled great houses at Chaco Canyon, but in contrast were invariably short-lived. The upland period was not a time of true abundance. Conditions changed far too rapidly and erratically to offer the stability and security of the early to middle Chaco period.

On this point, the condition of skeletal remains is telling. Infant mortality, although the data are sketchy, was likely much higher in the Pajarito villages than in the Chacoan great houses, where roughly 9 percent of all children died before the age of five. Still, it was probably lower than in the Red Mesa Valley farmsteads of the 1050s, where the infant death rate was a stunning 50 percent. Malnutrition, skeletal fragility resulting from insufficient calcium, incompletely mended bone breaks, seriously decayed and abscessed teeth, and other afflictions all show up again on the Pajarito, as they did among Chacoan farmers nearly two centuries earlier.

Researchers disagree over just why the final chapter of the upland period proved so fragile. Far to the south, recurring droughts struck the ancient Aztec world; their written records confirm that this collective "great drought" prevailed in central Mexico between 1276 and 1299. In the U.S. Southwest, the presence of mesa-top villages with reservoirs and cobble-mulched gardens over a large part of the northern Rio Grande tends to support the view that some droughts worked hardships on the Pajarito, too, at that time. Contributors to the ground-breaking book *Environmental Change and Human Adaptation in the Ancient American Southwest*, edited by David E. Doyel and Jeffrey S. Dean and published in 2006 by the University of Utah Press, have refined many of the climate details for this drought-plagued period.

In any case, drought is relative to average precipitation. The lower, eastern flanks of the Pajarito average eleven to about thirteen inches of precipitation a year. In much of the east-facing higher elevations, fifteen to twenty inches is the norm. Lose three or four inches of this precipitation and agriculture slips from being merely dicey to disastrous. Even such apparently small variations also affect the production of grass seeds, piñon nuts, and acorns, which were essential to the foraging component of the ancient Southwesterners' daily economy. Thus it is no surprise that Pajarito people experimented with pumice fields, artificial terracing, and rudimentary irrigation canals in the late 1200s.

Other archaeological facts should be considered in the debate over drought. If probable dates of abandonment are plotted geographically—ideally, from tree-ring-dated roof beams, and otherwise from pottery—for a hundred villages of the late 1200s at Mesa Verde, in the El Morro district, in the Gallina highlands, on the Pajarito Plateau, and in the Manzano Mountains southeast of Albuquerque, a singular fact emerges: ancient farming districts on the drier, western or southwestern slopes of mountain ranges were generally abandoned twenty to thirty years earlier in the 1200s than those on the moister, east-facing land masses. Bandelier and the Pajarito slope to the east, making it a natural refuge. The high mesas at El Morro and Mesa Verde were vacated *before* the wooded mesas at Bandelier or the east slopes of the Sandia Mountains at Albuquerque, fifty miles to the south. Indeed, some population probably shifted from El Morro and Mesa Verde to the Zuni and Pajarito districts as the droughts created havoc.

Clearly, the reliability of rain and snowfall was a significant factor between 1260 and 1300. But other sources of fragility could easily have been the uplands' shorter growing seasons and cool nighttime temperatures, coupled with the effects of a century and a half of hunting and wood-cutting in the ancient Southwest's most densely populated region. Such use-related factors narrowed the margins for environmental error. For example, the longer one farmed in a given place, the greater the risk of soil depletion.

A final factor might have been the straw that broke the upland model of efficiency formed on the Pajarito Plateau between 1150 and 1250. Both architecture (kivas) and changing patterns of ceramic trade in the later 1200s suggest that a second wave of immigration from the Mesa Verde area took place just as the Pajarito population was peaking. Such an influx could have rapidly pushed population density beyond the local carrying capacity and, coupled with even moderate droughts, destabilized the Pajarito's thirteenth-century adaptation to the upland environment. Such an influx would also have exerted pressure on farmers to expand their horticultural exploitation into any remaining unused, and less optimal, upland niches. We already know the consequences of this strategy in Chacoan times, and the risks were even greater in the uplands, with their short growing seasons. Did such pressure, coupled with drought, intensify the use of high-elevation grid gardens and cobble-mulch and pumice fields in the late 1200s? It is certainly plausible.

Few villages built on the Pajarito Plateau during the upland period, except for some of the cliff houses and large pueblos along permanent streams, were inhabited for long. Most were lived in, vacated, renovated, and then vacated again. By 1290, this cyclical pattern was broken, and the late-blossoming upland period on the Pajarito and in Bandelier began to disintegrate rapidly, once temporary moves metamorphosed into longer-term ones. By 1290 to 1300, a number of the large mesa-top plaza sites were already largely vacated, and people again scattered. This scattering, given the dense upland population and deteriorating conditions, verged on the predictable, but its specific nature tells us more. As some people left, other local groups merely moved into less desirable and less densely populated uplands and attempted to carry on in smaller settlements. One example may be Tijeras Pueblo, in the lower mountains above Albuquerque. Founded in the late 1200s, it struggled into the 1310–1315 period even as other villagers moved into lower, riverine settings. Like some sites on the Pajarito, Tijeras Pueblo was vacated, then resettled in the 1330s to 1350s. Such upland hangers-on were soon to become the minority. Many more people started new settlements in nearby "lowlands" around Santa Fe and in the Galisteo Basin while others, as at Tyuonyi, resettled in the best-watered upland canyon bottoms during the same years.

The new, lower-elevation settlements began with the construction of shallow, rectangular pithouses—not masonry and adobe pueblos— as if formally announcing another major chapter in Rio Grande history. Strangely, even as the mesa-top population declined in the upper elevations at

Bandelier, as elsewhere in the uplands, some of the Pajarito's most famous sites of the 1300s and 1400s were being founded. Many Pueblo peoples experimented with new village locations at the dawn of the Rio Grande Classic period in the early 1300s, but virtually all those who prospered settled along permanent, usually lower-elevation streams or rivers. In Bandelier, the mesa-top villages of Yapashi and San Miguel were permanently abandoned by the 1400s. Tyuonyi, on the banks of Frijoles Creek, not only survived but prospered.

At the end of the upland period, as at the fall of Chaco, another great trading network collapsed. By the 1290s, the beautiful red-and-black St. Johns Polychrome bowls were no longer available as trade wares from the Arizona uplands. This is crucial information for dating the dissolution of the upland adaptation, which had been two centuries in the making.

What was accomplished during the 160 years spent in the Pajarito's ponderosa and piñon forests after the fall of Chaco Canyon? The survivors learned society-saving lessons of efficiency, diversification in their food economy, and highly mixed farming techniques adapted to a wide variety of existing soil, temperature, and elevational microniches. The uplanders rediscovered ancient and crucial keys to sustainability that, with modifications and refinements, worked on a much larger scale than the cruder innovations of their Basketmaker ancestors five centuries earlier.

These adaptations included infrastructure investments not in roads and lavish great houses but in using and enhancing a new landscape's capacity to feed people. Survival meant working with, rather than against, the forces and limitations of nature. To do this, labor once invested in "big-box," Chaco-style projects was instead invested in water control features, small reservoirs, low-cost irrigation, cobble grid gardens, pumice mulch, terraced hillsides, and a much more diverse repertoire of cultigens. Whereas Chaco had approached its age's definition of monocropping, the uplanders worked feverishly at horticultural diversity, fully using the landscape. They also avoided rigid, formulaic responses to new and changing conditions. Equally important, their architecture and the condition of their skeletons indicate that they did not re-create another society starkly divided between poor producers and well-off planners. What resulted were new themes in community organization and its broad integration into the economy. Population density, coupled with unpredictable precipitation and even modest droughts, undid them as they neared or possibly exceeded the Pajarito's carrying capacity.

Water, Land, and Economic Diversity

The Riverine Period

About 1300, Southwestern society once again reconfigured itself. In northern New Mexico, most archaeologists consider the appearance of glaze-painted pottery to be the hallmark of what they locally call the Rio Grande Classic period, a time when many people moved to the valleys of the Rio Grande and its tributaries. But more fundamental changes came about after 1300 than the mere replacement of carbon-painted, black-on-white bowls with pots decorated in lead glaze paint on yellow or red backgrounds. As noted in the previous chapter, domestic architecture once more shifted to the highly efficient pithouse, freeing up labor needed to establish new farm fields. After half a century or so of capricious, rapidly fluctuating circumstances in the uplands, greater stability was the goal.

In the late 1200s, late upland society reassessed its possibilities, largely abandoning both high mesas and the dry-farming of mesa tops for the more certain horticultural techniques of canyon-bottom and floodplain farming and small-scale irrigation. Lower-than-average and more variable precipitation during the late 1200s diminished wild seed production in the uplands, forcing greater intensification of corn farming. That intensification was limited in the uplands by short growing seasons, cool nighttime temperatures, thin soils, nutrient deficiencies in the pumice fields, and droughts. Hence the downhill shift at about 1280 to 1320. With few exceptions, rivers and dependable creeks throughout the Southwest drew farmers downhill and away from the more remote uplands. Consequently, it is more sensible to think of this as a geographically widespread riverine period than as solely a Rio Grande period.

Although farmers had practiced effective irrigation during the heyday of the Chaco and Mimbres societies in the eleventh century, they did so mostly in the larger, richer settlements, where more labor was available. Irrigation did not become the norm in smaller communities until nearly three hundred years later. As ancestral Pueblo people responded to upland want, moved into lower elevations, and reorganized in the 1300s, the longer growing seasons in their new dwelling places made it worthwhile for them

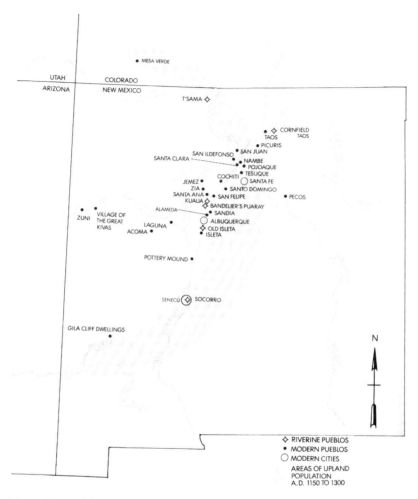

The modern pueblos and important ruins of the riverine period. Courtesy
Mary Powell/Ancient City Press.

to expand their farmable land, mostly within one to three quarters of a mile
of permanent streams and rivers. This expansion came with substantial
labor costs that could be mustered only after the small riverine pithouse
settlements of the early 1300s had been replaced by the growing masonry
and adobe pueblos of the 1320s through 1350s.

A generation after the move downhill from the piñon and ponderosa
forests at the end of the upland period, far more extensive terracing of
lower-elevation hillsides was being used to form flat garden plots, prevent

erosion, and slow runoff so that rainwater penetrated the soil. In northern New Mexico, grid gardens also gradually grew in size and complexity. The now desolate La Bajada Mesa, just southeast of Bandelier, once had large areas of neatly gridded garden plots and cornfields, which can still be seen clearly in aerial photographs. With the assistance of such infrastructure, some dry-farming was still practiced extensively as a crucial adjunct to stream- and irrigation-fed fields.

True irrigation canals were built in the lower elevations. Some of the springs and streams that rose on the Pajarito Plateau and in other uplands were diverted into small but effective stone-lined aqueducts, and elaborate irrigation systems were built up over the centuries. Some historians think of irrigation ditches, or acequias, as purely a Spanish innovation, but Pueblo peoples and archaeologists know that is not the case. These technical and architectural developments, however, which once earned the label "Rio Grande Classic," did not materialize immediately.

Life in the small, riverine pithouse settlements of the very early 1300s was not easy. Most of the former uplanders' infrastructural investments of the late 1200s had to be abandoned—an excruciating loss of the sweat equity they had invested in the Pajarito Plateau. Big-box infrastructure and landscape projects had become possible in the uplands only after small mesa-top villages had coalesced into larger communities that, depending on locale, merit the label "Coalition," "Great Pueblo," or "Pueblo III." But it had been the pattern of small communities, hard work, new efficiencies, and then growth that had ushered in the upland period, and now, in the first half of the 1300s, that pattern was repeated.

The early riverine pithouse communities, like tiny Pueblo Encierro, built in places such as Cochiti Reservoir, possessed the hard-won knowledge of labor-costly infrastructure. But their investment was locked up on the high mesas in an environment that could no longer sustain everyone. As a result, pithouse builders of the early 1300s lost the momentum of the late upland period and had to start over. For the average settler, that meant low-intensity horticulture, a modest investment in housing, disrupted trade networks, planting new fields in new microenvironments, and foraging the game-rich river basins, all with little of the community support that might have been gained through the labor pool of a large pueblo. Judging from the modest architecture built between 1300 and 1320, it was in new farm fields that scarce labor was disproportionately invested.

With the major changes in environment and style of agriculture came other, later waves of movement into or out of the uplands and local riverine districts. Emerging territories again overlapped, just as they had after the Chacoan decline, creating social tensions and leaving the geographic distribution of language groups an even more complicated mosaic than before. Just when the uplands around Mesa Verde, El Morro, and Gila Cliff Dwellings National Monument were largely abandoned, by 1300 the riverine period in the northern Rio Grande and at the lower elevations of Bandelier Monument involved crowding and competition that must have been sufficient to induce local conflicts. Archaeologist Steven LeBlanc summarized the pertinent data about recurring conflicts in his book *Prehistoric Warfare in the Southwest.*

These tensions may have led to the construction of the compact masonry citadels that appeared on hills and mesas along the Rio Grande between La Bajada Mesa and the modern town of Belen by the 1320s. Although their masonry is coarser and their scale smaller, these little-studied, sometimes multistory sites echo the fortified granaries of the upland period that were once constructed as part of the great cliff houses. Whether the citadels of the early 1300s stood alone, as self-contained settlements, or functioned as the fortified, postharvest, winter refuges of nearby pithouse dwellers along the Rio Grande is unknown. Some version of the latter interpretation is attractive, for it had been only fifty to seventy-five years since the abandoned cliff houses were still being built and expanded, and cultural habits are powerful.

By the 1320s, the construction of shallow, rectangular pithouses had been replaced by the building of modest farmsteads of adobe, jacal, or masonry, depending on locally available materials. The small hilltop citadels were in use, and trade in the new lead-glazed Rio Grande polychromes was expanding rapidly along rivers and creeks. The trade connected upstream and downstream communities in long, spaghetti-like trading districts, within which one or another portion of the population seems always to have been moving temporarily upriver or downriver—"following the rains," as Pueblo elders still phrase it today.

Hidden in the archaeological confusion of the early fourteenth century are also fascinating regularities. The earliest riverine pueblos were modest in size and situated on easily fortified hillsides above rivers such as the Chama and the Rio Grande. Pueblo peoples generally moved south and east out of southwestern Colorado, altogether abandoning the Mesa Verde district, the northern San Juan Basin, and Colorado's Montezuma Valley. At the same time, Mogollon people in what is now the Gila National Forest moved either downstream along the Gila River (southwest into Arizona), northeast along the lower Rio Grande corridor, or eastward, pushing into the small basins across the southern quarter of New Mexico. The last are archaeologically labeled as the territory of the "Jornada-Mogollon" people, who are thought to have been poor, backward cousins of the Mogollon-Mimbres people of the upper Gila River country.

The ancestral Pueblo population of New Mexico as a whole had probably declined sharply just after the fall of Chaco and again during the hardships of the late 1200s, when many uplanders died or moved on. Consequently, the most successful riverine farmers of the 1300s and 1400s were able to maintain access to relatively empty nearby mountain districts for foraging, hunting, and occasional drought-year farming. The net result of these changes was that by the mid- to late 1300s, there were again growing farming populations along northern New Mexico's rivers, from the Chama Valley south as far as the area around Socorro. Bandelier Monument and the Pajarito Plateau figured prominently in this geographical redistribution, because their land, religious sites, and even infrastructure were reused heavily by fourteenth- to sixteenth-century riverine period descendants when conditions dictated. The partial recapture of "abandoned" Pajarito land and infrastructure was crucial to riverine period success and survival, and it was integral to the continuing cultural efficiency that replaced the Chacoan period's obsession with growth and power.

In the 1300s, a few new pueblo-style villages were built on the Pajarito, even as the main thrust of Pueblo development continued to be focused on the rivers. Some of the pueblos founded in the 1320s or 1330s and later expanded were Yapashi, San Miguel, Tshirege, Tsankawi, Otowi, and Puye, several of which were built adjacent to earlier, smaller "sister" communities. Tyuonyi, situated in Frijoles Canyon on the banks of the east-flowing Frijoles Creek, was established a bit earlier than the pueblos just named but saw notable expansion in early riverine times.

These fourteenth-century pueblos, it can be argued, formed an important adaptational bridge between the upland and riverine periods, for they preserved access to the high country, illustrating the timeless rule of real estate: location, location, location. As a consequence, settlement patterns changed significantly by the mid-1300s. Other than in the riverside or streamside locations of the more numerous lower-elevation sites, one finds that in the lower floodplains and the resettled uplands, most large pueblos were surrounded by miles of scattered field houses in the 1300s to 1500s.

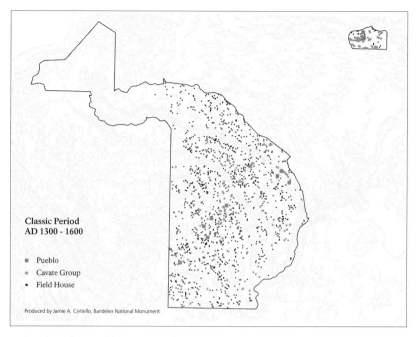

Archaeological sites of the riverine (Classic) period in Bandelier National Monument, 1300–1600. Courtesy Jamie Civitello and Bandelier National Monument.

Those field houses often consisted of two rooms, one for storage and one to sleep in, with rough rock walls and a make-do roof. Typically, they were tucked up against large boulders to give expedient shelter to people who spent the farming season next to fields miles from their main village. Instead of moving entire farmsteads and small villages—the pattern that had characterized the uplands from about 1150 to 1250—ancestral Pueblo people of the riverine period simply moved their fields and built field houses when necessary, at a much lower labor cost than resettling a village. And at all times they maximized horticultural diversity by farming an amazing variety of microniches spread across fifty to one hundred square miles. That diversity added to the stability of the riverine pueblos and became a key element in Pueblo survival over the ensuing centuries.

In the 1300s to 1500s, former Pajaritans enjoyed an important advantage that recent comers to the Rio Grande Valley might not have had. By using the large, late-founded pueblos such as Otowi, in and north of Bandelier Monument, as anchors, the descendants of upland period farmers maintained access to hundreds of square miles of foraging and hunting territory, along with many higher-elevation fields. Importantly, most of those fields had lain fallow for as much as four or five generations before being re-farmed during the Rio Grande Classic period, so they had recovered their soil nutrients. Such reuse of the Pajarito Plateau added immensely to horticultural diversity, compensated for drought years, secured access to large game in the high country (deer were favored), and placed field-house farmers where they could also forage for wild plants, including piñon nuts, acorns, and the still highly important grass seeds.

Existing upland fields, many of them terraced or cobble mulched 50 to 150 years before their Classic period reuse, were recaptured infrastructure, substantially reducing new labor investments. But the recycling of infrastructure did not stop with merely tidying up old fields. Many small, masonry, upland period farmsteads, including the Santa Fe Black-on-white pueblos of the late 1100s, were dismantled during the riverine period to provide the tuff blocks needed to extend old upland grid gardens, make new check dams, build the walls of field houses, and even make stone linings for the rudimentary aqueducts found in White Rock Canyon, just north of the monument.

Recapturing long-ago labor investments and using forces of nature such as gravity and the sun-heating of mulch were extremely efficient measures. As archaeologists Rory Gauthier and Cynthia Herhahn have pointed out, even the organic material trapped in the floors of old domestic structures and in nearby village waste middens was recaptured in the process of farming on top of old farmsteads. Similar reuse of upland infrastructure also took place in the Zuni area, in the Jemez Mountains, and, to a lesser extent, in the Taos district. The "green" revolution began long ago.

But the uplands were not the core focus of riverine period culture. By 1350, the initial political readjustment to another episode of mass migration had passed, and classic riverine society began to emerge. Immense, unfortified pueblos were built up in bottomlands along primary rivers and their tributaries. Some were constructed of coursed adobe, and others of stone. They were surrounded by hundreds of outlying field houses, used during the growing season. Like the upland field houses built during this period, those in the lower elevations also maximized horticultural diversity. Low mesas, dune fields, creek bottoms, terraced hillsides, and small side canyons emptying into the region's reliable streams and rivers were all used to extend the horticultural diversity in a pueblo's close-in fields. Rather like the trade networks that connected diverse localities into

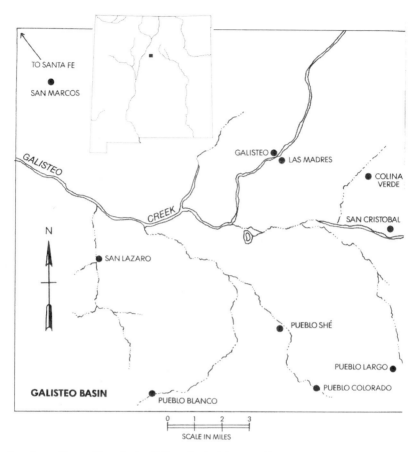

Locations of large villages in the Galisteo Basin. These pueblos are typical of the riverine, or Rio Grande Classic, period, 1300–1600. Courtesy Mary Powell/Ancient City Press.

a less risky whole, the farming pattern, too, followed the efficiency rule of spreading risks.

Yet nothing like Chaco's hugely powerful and expensive regional, political, and economic network ever again emerged. Each large pueblo became more like a miniature city-state or a semifortified town of feudal Europe. Population probably fluctuated during the repetitive cycles of rain and drought, and as best we know, primary loyalties were first to kin-based clans, then to special religious and curing societies, and then to the village. Pueblos alternately cooperated and competed with one another as circumstances dictated, much as they—and larger nations—do to this day.

The 1370s, the early and late 1400s, and the late 1500s were periods of intense droughts and episodes of highly variable precipitation. Both environmental scenarios bring small farmers to their knees. Coupled with the Southwest's enduringly patchy rainfall, the climate fluctuations required nearly constant adjustments to local farming conditions. And with each drought, upland farming temporarily intensified. The pueblos that had most successfully maintained access to adjacent uplands fared best. Many that had not simply did not make it into the 1500s, for the droughts of the later 1400s were brutal. Many villages went through several cycles of partial abandonment and renewal between 1325 and 1500. Occasionally, floods swept away precious bottomland, and local river areas were temporarily abandoned, only to be resettled and villages repaired a generation or so later. Archaeologists monitor these comings and goings most easily by studying the layers of floor deposits uncovered during excavations. It is rare for archaeologists to find a village or a major portion of one that was inhabited continuously, at what most of us think of as "normal occupancy rates," for any great length of time during the riverine period. Recurring soil depletions, as well as variations in precipitation and even social conflict, contributed to this pattern.

In spite of setbacks and uncertainty, Classic riverine society was much more stable than upland society had been and produced significant accomplishments in technology, the arts, and religion. In addition to new techniques of pottery manufacture, a large variety of more efficient tools was introduced to portions of the Bandelier area that were reused in the 1300s, 1400s, and early 1500s. Beautifully shaped stone axes of unusual hardness were fashioned from large river cobbles. Some of these have three-quarter spiral hafting grooves, an effective innovation for tightly securing the ax head to a handle. Even in modern times, an ax handle tends to separate from the head because of tremendous impact pressures and centrifugal forces created by the wide overhead swing favored by woodsmen the world over.

All manner of small tools were created from wood, bone, stone, and pottery. Wooden artifacts of this period have usually decayed over the centuries, so archaeologists most often find the more durable materials. Animal bones were used for everything from whistles and small flutes to intricate sewing needles and sets of incising tools. Manos and metates were large and efficient, often set up in rows of coarse to fine stones in areas known as "mealing bins," where women gathered to talk or sing and grind corn in a modest assembly line. This practice, too, was efficient.

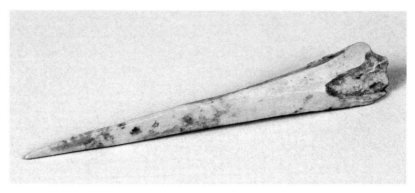

Bone awl found at Rainbow House, on the southern Pajarito Plateau. Rabbit, turkey, and deer bones were important raw materials for small tools made throughout the ancient Southwest over a span of five thousand to eleven thousand years. Courtesy National Park Service, Bandelier National Monument.

The weaving of native cotton into intricate sashes and belts also became a high art form, and fragments of the textiles have survived. Their quality, considering that the weavers used hand looms and hand-sorted cotton fibers (there were no ginning or carding machines), is utterly amazing.

Pottery, too, reached new heights in form, style, and versatility. Artisans produced everything from fired clay pendants to tobacco pipes, and from ollas, or large kitchen jars, to elaborate miniature sets of finely painted bowls. Certain villages, such as Kewa (Santo Domingo) Pueblo and the long-abandoned Tonque Pueblo, both near Interstate 25 between Albuquerque and Santa Fe, began to specialize in pottery manufacture. Much of what is known about fourteenth- and fifteenth-century life in areas bordering Bandelier is owed to microscopic analyses of the kinds of ground materials —usually stone—that potters used to temper their clay pastes.

The technique of glazing pottery had been known in the Four Corners area since at least 400 or 500 CE. The early glaze-decorated wares were black-on-whites glazed with iron silica. During the riverine period, most of the Rio Grande glaze-ware styles used a lead-based glaze. Lead-bearing ores were obtained from deposits of galena and similar minerals from several nearby mining districts. One of the most important of these was near the present-day village of Cerrillos, about twenty miles southeast of the Pajarito Plateau, where turquoise has also been mined since ancient times. Other deposits are still owned by one or another of the surviving pueblos, whose members guard their knowledge of the locations, both to protect the resources and to show veneration to the ancestors who mined them by hand.

Some of the earliest Rio Grande glaze wares are types called Agua Fria Glaze-on-red and, nearer to Albuquerque, Los Padillas Glaze Polychrome. Agua Fria Glaze-on-red was produced at Pueblo Kuapa (LA 3444), on the southern Pajarito Plateau a few miles south of Bandelier. But within a few years, two separate glaze pottery traditions had evolved. The most widespread one was characterized by dark designs glazed on a red background. The other, more limited in geographical distribution, was glaze-on-yellow pottery. Both were handcrafted on the Pajarito Plateau after the upland period, with the yellows more common south of the monument.

By tracing the crushed stone used for tempering the clays, a rough outline of economics and changes in settlement can be pieced together for the Bandelier area. In the 1300s, only Tyuonyi and Rainbow House, in Frijoles Canyon, produced glaze ware. At the southern end of the monument, San Miguel Pueblo (LA 370) and Yapashi (LA 250), near the Shrine of the Stone Lions, produced some glaze-on-yellows.

Tyuonyi's glaze-on-reds were often tempered with crushed red volcanic scoria, a stone still commonly used in landscaping throughout northern New Mexico. But pottery from Tyuonyi did not enjoy much trade over any great distance. By the late 1300s, the focus of pottery trade in Rio Grande society had shifted eastward, toward Santa Fe and the Galisteo Basin. In the mid-fifteenth century, the villages of San Miguel and Las Casas, in Bandelier Monument, were largely abandoned. Yapashi, probably founded sometime in the late 1200s and expanded later, no longer produced pottery and was no doubt in the process of abandonment. In the monument, that left only Tyuonyi producing some glaze ware, with crushed tuff temper from local volcanic deposits.

To the north of Frijoles Canyon in the mid-1300s, the Tewa sites of Otowi, Tsankawi, and Tsirege began to produce or to import their first glaze wares in quantity, complementing the local black-on-gray wares. The northward spread of glaze ware never really proceeded further. No one is certain when Otowi was established. It was excavated in 1916 and 1917, and on the basis of pottery styles, most of its excavated rooms were found to date from the mid-fourteenth to the sixteenth century. It reached its greatest size in the late 1400s to mid-1500s. But pottery dating to the late 1200s and early 1300s comes from a small sister site nearby, which

An Agua Fria Glaze-on-red pot of the early riverine period.
Courtesy Michael P. Marshall, Maxwell Museum Collections.

A bowl of a type called Galisteo Black-on-white, typical of the black-on-white pottery that continued to be manufactured south of the Pajarito Plateau between 1300 and 1400, even though glaze wares became more common. Courtesy Michael P. Marshall, Maxwell Museum Collections.

suggests that an earlier component might also lie beneath Otowi itself. Unfortunately, the excavations were conducted with methods that answer few current questions. Tsankawi, on its spectacular mesa in the northern part of the monument, was founded earlier and served as an upland anchor during the succeeding riverine period.

The late 1400s to mid-1500s were a time of master craftspeople who generated the objects that once induced archaeologists and museum curators to dub their era, and their work, "Classic." In Europe, the Renaissance phenomenon of art and master craftsmen arose largely because of plague-induced labor scarcities in the preceding centuries. After the plagues, labor and true craft skills increased sharply in value. If, as I suspect, the northern Southwest saw substantial population losses in the 1100s, in the late 1200s, and again during the severe droughts of the 1400s, that might explain why the early to mid-1500s were a time of large villages and great craftspeople even while communities continued to eschew the kinds of monumental projects that had once dragged at the Chacoans.

Continued studies will eventually permit an even more detailed reconstruction of the Classic period on the Pajarito Plateau, but the basic facts are the following. After 1300, although some people remained on the plateau at sites such as Tyuonyi, Yapashi, San Miguel, and Las Casas, the main focus of Classic period society moved downhill, east and south, out of Bandelier and the Pajarito. In the monument itself, only Tyuonyi and Rainbow House in the north and San Miguel and Yapashi in the south housed permanent populations; most of the smaller sites at higher elevations above the Rio Grande had been abandoned. Then, in the early 1400s, again in the late 1400s, and a third time in the late 1500s, a portion of the regional population once more concentrated in a few large, higher-elevation sites such as Otowi, Tsirege, Puye, and Tsankawi, on the plateau well to the north of Bandelier Monument. Rainbow House had already been abandoned by year-round residents by this time.

The riverine, or Rio Grande Classic, period is far more complex than many textbooks indicate. Several major reorganizations and episodes of mass population movement had taken place well before the Spaniards arrived—first the explorer Francisco Vázquez de Coronado in 1540–1541 and actual settlers in 1598. In the late 1400s and again in the mid- to late 1500s, serious droughts forced major episodes of abandonment, followed by relocation and rebuilding in areas where farmland was still abundant. Bandelier and the Pajarito Plateau, like the high mesas above modern-day

Jemez Pueblo, remained a safety valve throughout—upland refuges rich in game, valuable obsidian, old infrastructure to recycle, and seasonal crops of berries, grasses, acorns, and piñon nuts. They were places where entire clans could relocate in times of drought or of conflict.

Unlike during earlier periods in Southwestern history, from the riverine period onward the most successful lowland pueblos never again divorced themselves from adjacent mountain retreats. Nearly all those that did not hold unshared access to mountain land, such as the well-studied but west-slope-sited pueblo of Arroyo Hondo south of Santa Fe, failed to survive the severe droughts of the 1400s. Although the pueblos in Bandelier had been completely abandoned before actual Spanish colonization, succeeding Indian peoples continued to use the Pajarito, worshipped within its confines, reused its field houses and farmed it occasionally, hunted in it annually, considered it part of their rightful territory, and venerated it as an ancestral home. This deep sense of home place is difficult for non-Indian, post–World War II Americans to understand.

Even religion changed during the Classic period. A new cult flourished that was centered on kachinas—masked gods associated with rain. Most scholars agree that the kachina religion originated in the Zuni area or a bit farther west. Kiva murals reached a zenith in beauty and symbolism and in complex portrayals of religious characters and events. Even petroglyphs, or "rock art," were laboriously hand-pecked in the recognizable "Rio Grande style." Many such petroglyphs can still be seen at Bandelier Monument and in canyons to both the north and south. A particularly notable concentration of Rio Grande–style rock art overlooking Albuquerque has become Petroglyph National Monument.

Daily life during the riverine period was rich and varied but always arduous. Men worked the soil and were weavers and craftsmen in stone. Women cooked, made pottery, tended to the annual replastering of house walls, and cared for children. Men were heavily involved in kiva society and the ritual life of the village. They cut roof beams, hunted, repaired house roofs, and stood night watch. Women formed the fabric of home life, nurturing the several generations who usually lived under one roof. Whereas sex roles were sharply divided, no real division existed between sacred and secular. Religion was not merely a once-a-week event, a few hours of reverence in the midst of an everyday world. Rather, daily life and religion were constructed more like an onion: it took many layers of each to produce the complex whole of Pueblo society.

Petroglyphs on a rock jutting into a pool of water in a small canyon on the east side of the
Rio Grande—a typical setting for petroglyphs carved in the Rio Grande style after 1300.
Courtesy of Rory Gauthier.

Many of these traditions continue in modern times. In Pueblo reli-
gions, mountains are sacred, and specific mountains are very sacred.
Indian peoples still maintain sacred shrines in and around Bandelier.
Archaeologists and visitors consider the Stone Lions a "site," but the
Pueblos consider the hewn rocks a living shrine. From surprising distances, people still come quietly and reverently, on foot, to this sacred
high place. The lions are best considered an altar within a great natural
cathedral. Indeed, the lions themselves, like many other shrines on the
Pajarito, are a source of power and hope. It took people both qualities
to survive nearly six hundred generations of uncertain life in and around
Bandelier, but they did so.

Indeed, Bandelier and the Pajarito Plateau have served Pueblo society
well. It was there that the densest human populations in any Southwestern
district until modern times sought refuge after the fall and fragmentation
of Chacoan society. It was there that the sustaining lessons of efficiency
were relearned and refined in the 1100s and 1200s, under indelibly painful

circumstances. And it was there that the general value of efficiency was transformed by constant experimentation, hard work, and sheer cultural grit into effective, on-the-ground models of the way to pursue sustainability through ecological and economic diversity. It was also there that surviving Rio Grande Pueblo society acquired its enduring distaste for grandiose public infrastructure and its obsession with practical, productive community projects such as creating grid gardens, horticultural terraces, and irrigation systems. Finally, it was on the Pajarito Plateau that the lavish Chacoan costs of radical class differences were rejected, to be replaced by a more highly integrated social order with an economic diversity so muted that archaeologists cannot, unlike at Chaco Canyon, detect statistically useful class differences from buried skeletal remains alone.

Had Bandelier and the Pajarito not served first as a post-Chaco refuge and then as a crucible in which knowledge was recast into a model of long-term sustainability during the 1100s to 1300s—and had they not again served as a refuge during the Pueblo Revolt (against Hispanic settlers) of 1680 to 1692—there might have been no Rio Grande Pueblo society equipped to survive what was to come. Descendants of the first desperate Chaco-era farmers to reach the Pajarito are now entering the tenth century of their post-apocalypse life. They will be among my students when I teach the course "Ancient New Mexico" and explain just why drives for power and growth must be balanced with efficiency and moderation if a society aspires to win the game of evolutionary survival over the long haul. I find that Native American students are the ones who most commonly understand and identify with this message. As for the other students, I am always curious to see how they respond as inheritors of years of corporate greed, amateurishly unsustainable power, and growth-based business models that have visited economic catastrophe on millions of ordinary families. My hope is that lessons of efficiency learned on the Pajarito Plateau will seem immediate and meaningful to all of them.

Postscript

The practical implications of what took place on the Pajarito Plateau and in what is now Bandelier National Monument reach far beyond what one might imagine. The most obvious take-away message from this book is that the Tewa and Keres world survived in no small part because those peoples managed to redirect their fragmented, post-Chaco society along a trajectory of ecological and horticultural diversity bound to efficient behaviors.

Most of us probably assume that their survival is a niche issue in the totality of modern America. Nothing could be farther from the truth. We have seen unquenchable greed and epic stupidity induce economic wreckage in the world twice during the last hundred years: during the Great Depression of the 1930s and during what is being called, at the time I write, the Great Recession of 2008–2010. Just like the ancients, we "moderns" must adapt to resource scarcities and climate changes that will not fully reverse themselves in our time—possibly not even in our children's.

We face essentially the same issues that were faced at the end of Chacoan society and recast in the uplands of the Southwest between 1150 and 1290. As modern Americans in a fragile society, we need to learn every possible detail of those dynamics. We, too, need to find ways to diversify our economy, overcome the national tendency to be grandiose, and build infrastructure that will harness, rather than fight, the forces of nature. We must make waste a far rarer occurrence. We need a sophisticated rebalancing that ordinary Americans can forge through their daily decisions—driving a fuel-efficient car, using cooler, low-energy light bulbs, taking more public transportation, and easing up on the energetically lavish and environmentally destructive desire for corn-fed, feedlot meat. Perhaps above all we need to learn that the class of Americans who most like to lead us is too often the product of great power and great wealth. We cannot afford them, and we cannot count on their stilted and detached worldview to set a balanced and safe direction for our next century.

Further research into life in Bandelier National Monument and on the Pajarito Plateau during the twelfth through fifteenth centuries will tell us even more than has already been learned. That means precision-targeted excavations at selected upland sites of the 1100s, the mid-1200s, and the decades from 1280 through the 1320s, as well as at pueblos that grew about the time of the droughts in the 1400s. Just how did the Pueblo Indians collapse a social hierarchy of at least three tiered classes in the Chacoan world—the canyon great-house elites, the second-tier outlier great-house elites, and the common farmers—into a much more egalitarian and far less costly social system by the early 1500s? We need this knowledge, and we need it sooner rather than later.

PART THREE

Gifts
from the
Past

Long House Ruin in 1964. Courtesy National Park Service, Bandelier National Monument.

Long House Ruin in 2006. Erosion since the earlier photograph was taken has been dramatic. Courtesy National Park Service, Bandelier National Monument.

Tyuonyi

The ruins of Tyuonyi are the archaeological centerpiece of Bandelier National Monument. The village formed a tangible bridge between the upland period, which ended about 1300, and the subsequent riverine, or Rio Grande Classic, period. Tyuonyi was probably founded in the late thirteenth century, but much of what visitors see now was built between roughly 1350 and 1425 or 1450. Its building episodes correlate roughly with droughts in the 1300s and horrendous ones in the 1400s. Such conditions intensified the use of the uplands as horticultural safety valves for residents of Rio Grande pueblos who farmed in the lower elevations to the east.

Tyuonyi is a rough, masonry oval similar to other villages, such as Soldado Ruin west of El Morro National Monument, that were founded about the same time and at nearly the same elevation. Tier upon tier of rooms were built around the central plaza until the pueblo assumed its final form. Some archaeologists believe the final building episode involved construction of the narrower tiers, only three or four rooms deep, that face Frijoles Creek. These tiers, they argue, transformed Tyuonyi into the enclosed, easily defended oval that is seen today.

We may never know precisely, because this ruin was excavated between 1908 and 1911 by Edgar Lee Hewett, who founded what are now the School for Advanced Research and the Museum of New Mexico in Santa Fe. In those days, the modern dating techniques essential to re-creating a pueblo's expansion, room by room, were still unknown. Roof beam fragments collected thirty years or more after Hewett's excavations were analyzed and dated at the University of Arizona's Laboratory of Tree-Ring Research—the world's authority on tree-ring dating—but those fragments accurately date only a few rooms. Pieces of beams originally from upper floors are mixed in with those from lower floors, which were built first. To complicate matters, sound roof timbers were often carried away after a village was vacated and reused several times to build a succession of Puebloan structures. Perhaps one day, when the time is right, the National Park

Tyuonyi, looking south, with Frijoles Creek in the background. Note the absence of cliff rooms on the north face of Frijoles Canyon. Courtesy National Park Service, Bandelier National Monument.

Service will authorize archaeologists to investigate the still unexcavated portion of Tyuonyi, where the contemporary trail through the ruin exits over ancient walls.

Six hundred years ago, Frijoles Creek ran much closer to the ruin's south walls than it does today. Indeed, long-ago floods may have taken away some of Tyuonyi's southernmost walls. In its day, Tyuonyi was rather like a fortress. In its final form, only a narrow entryway to the east opened to the great plaza. Plaster made of mud and ash covered the masonry walls, and access to most ground-floor rooms was by ladder to the roof, then down through rooftop openings.

At its zenith, Tyuonyi's more than four hundred rooms, three kivas, and retaining walls along the creek created an impressive village. Pottery was manufactured locally for many generations. Although Tyuonyi did not hold economic influence over a large geographic area, it sat in an important frontier between Tewa speakers to the north and, to the south, Keres speakers, who claim the pueblo today as one of their ancestral homes. The frontier is most obvious in the different types of pottery

A riverine period bowl of the kind known as biscuit ware, from the northern Pajarito Plateau, about 1350–1450. Courtesy Michael P. Marshall, Maxwell Museum Collections.

found on either side of it: predominantly Tewa carbon-painted, black-on-white biscuit wares to the north, and Keres glaze-decorated wares to the south. Tyuonyi is still remembered in the rich oral traditions of both peoples, but its strongest ties by far are with modern, Keres-speaking Cochiti Pueblo.

Another, unexcavated pueblo of about twenty rooms lies between Tyuonyi and the Big Kiva near the visitor center. Its precise age is unknown. The Big Kiva was last repaired in 1513. No one knows just when Tyuonyi was completely abandoned, but the mid- to late 1500s is a likely period because the village produced no pottery after that time. Tyuonyi is particularly impressive when viewed from Ruin Overlook, on the mesa above it, and when winter snow highlights its intricate, now eroded outline on the floor of Frijoles Canyon.

Talus House and Long House

Talus House is nestled against the north cliff face of Frijoles Canyon, upstream from Tyuonyi. Most of its shallow, shadowed cave rooms, gouged out of the cliff with stone hand-tools, were originally the back rooms of upper stories. Below the cave rooms lies a part of Talus House that the National Park Service has reconstructed to give visitors an idea of what a small cliff house was like seven hundred years ago. During the 1930s this section was partially rebuilt from local tuff blocks. Even the original holes for roof beams, which had been pecked into the cliff face hundreds of years ago, were reused. Judging from pottery collected below Talus House a century ago, it appears to have been renovated again and again in ancient times. Exact dates are unknown, but it was probably not used much before 1200 and quite likely was lived in until Tyuonyi was abandoned. In 1909, Edgar Hewett referred to this cliff ruin as "Sun House," a name not used in many years.

Talus House, 1922. Ninety years of erosion of the tuff cliff face have partially erased the former features of this site, like so many others. These soft rock faces are very fragile. Courtesy National Park Service, Bandelier National Monument.

Long House, 1912. Note the good preservation in parts of the ruin. Courtesy National Park Service, Bandelier National Monument.

Long House, 1964. There is continual erosion of cave rooms in the cliff face relative to 1912 photographs. Courtesy National Park Service, Bandelier National Monument.

Long House sits approximately one-quarter mile upstream from Tyuonyi, beyond Talus House. It is one of the largest, longest, most complex structures on the Pajarito Plateau. At Long House, eight hundred feet of soft cliff face supported nearly three hundred rooms, three stories high in some places. The roof beam sockets dug into the cliff face are particularly noticeable. Long House, too, was rebuilt several times, but no modern study of its artifacts has been undertaken since it was excavated in the early 1900s. It had several kivas and could have housed a population of several hundred. Test excavations into the talus slope beneath it could still tell us more, as could reanalysis of its artifacts. This is a doctoral dissertation waiting to happen, especially if the site is compared carefully with Talus House and Tyuonyi.

Frijolito Ruin

On the south mesa overlooking Tyuonyi lies Frijolito Ruin. Excavated by the legendary archaeologist A. V. Kidder (though not to his later standards) while he was still a student of Edgar Hewett's, it is sometimes said to have been contemporaneous with Rainbow House, which dates to around 1200 CE. More likely, Frijolito Ruin was founded in the late 1200s; it is typical of the larger, more complex Santa Fe Black-on-white pueblos that survived into early glaze-ware times. Based on the pottery found at Frijolito Ruin, it was undoubtedly abandoned before Tyuonyi and Rainbow House. That makes sense, because thin mesa soils lose their organic matter to erosion while the canyon bottoms below gain eroded nutrients. Thus, fields in the canyons can often be farmed longer. Frijolito contains between seventy and eighty rooms, and as at many other Santa Fe Black-on-white sites, no ceremonial kiva is visible. Its heyday preceded Tyuonyi's greatest period of growth (the mid-1300s), and it might have been linked to Long House or Talus House. We need to know more.

Ceremonial Cave and Alcove House

High on the north cliff face, nearly a mile upstream from Tyuonyi, is a spectacular, reconstructed kiva inside Ceremonial Cave. To reach the cave—actually a large rock overhang—one must scale Park Service–provided ladders up the canyon wall to a height of nearly 150 feet above Frijoles Creek, a breathtaking experience. Inside the overhang there were once nearly thirty small masonry rooms, in places two stories high—a pueblo now called Alcove House. Dug into the floor of the cave was a small kiva, entered from the roof. Now reconstructed, it gives visitors a good idea of what a local kiva was like.

For generations, archaeologists have been confused by the details of kiva construction on the Pajarito Plateau. When excavated, many kivas show a complex combination of features similar to those of kivas in either the Chaco or Mesa Verde area and features that resulted from local experimentation. Using these details, researchers have sought to unravel the "whens and wheres" of the various migrations to the Pajarito after 1150. Most likely it will require far more excavation on the plateau and far more attention to the precise dating of ruins in and around Frijoles Canyon before we have refined answers. Most archaeologists agree that features of both Chaco and Mesa Verde kivas show up on the Pajarito, but details vary from one kiva to another even in a single village, as is demonstrated at the sites in Frijoles Canyon. Other hamlets, such as some of the early Santa Fe Black-on-white sites, have no kivas at all. The lingering questions of "who, when, and where" beg to be answered through DNA evidence rather than architectural inference.

The Alcove House kiva is small and simple, like many others in the northern Rio Grande Valley. Because the cave's location is the most easily defensible one in all of Frijoles Canyon, the pueblo inside it was probably built about 1200, during the heyday of similar, easily defended "cliff palaces" throughout the Southwest. Later cliff dwellings on the Pajarito were often less well situated for defense, but they retained all the other efficiency advantages of the earlier cliff houses.

Ceremonial Cave, named by Edgar Hewett in the early 1900s, held a habitation site, now called Alcove House, with an associated kiva. Part of the reconstructed kiva can be seen at lower right in the photograph, with a person emerging through the roof entry. Courtesy National Park Service, Bandelier National Monument.

Directly below Alcove House and across the canyon floor, on the south side of Frijoles Creek, lies a small ruin from the late upland period—elsewhere called Pueblo III. First noted by Adolph Bandelier and rather romantically called House of the Water People, it is ten to fifteen rooms in size, unexcavated, and seldom mentioned. It probably was built about the same time as Alcove House. It contains traces of red and black polychromes from western New Mexico and fragments of early Santa Fe Black-on-white pottery. That places it in the period from 1150 or 1175 to 1250 CE. No kiva is obvious at House of the Water People, so it might be an early pueblo with close connections to Ceremonial Cave, or it might simply be typical of the larger Santa Fe Black-on-white sites. If so, were the missing kivas for those sites separate community ones that doubled as temporary refuges in times of conflict? There is still much to be discovered here.

Yapashi

Yapashi Pueblo sits atop the mesa south of Alamo Canyon. It is quite a trek from the visitor center, but a worthwhile one for hiking enthusiasts. Alamo Canyon lies south of monument headquarters, separated from Frijoles Canyon by Lummis Canyon. There the vegetation changes from the ponderosa pine forest found around Tyuonyi to piñon-juniper parkland.

Yapashi Pueblo was large—several stories tall with hundreds of rooms—and probably was an important Keres village before the southern Pajarito Plateau was abandoned in the early 1500s. Modern Cochiti Indians regard it as an ancestral home. Edgar Hewett excavated there briefly in 1908 but never published an adequate report. From pottery found at Yapashi, Hewett dated the site between 1200 and 1475. Unfortunately, this tells us little about the dynamics of survival and adaptation that Yapashi represents. In any case, much of its glaze ware appears to have been trade goods acquired from San Marcos Pueblo, in the Galisteo Basin, and from Tonque Pueblo, between Albuquerque and Santa Fe. We now know more about the dates of pottery manufacture than Hewett did, and this information suggests that Yapashi flourished in the mid-1300s and again in the 1400s, with a diminished population between those drought-driven peaks. Yapashi is a Keres name that refers to the sacred enclosure around the nearby Shrine of the Stone Lions.

Part of the remnants of Yapashi. Photograph probably taken by Charles Lummis, late 1800s. The walls no longer stand this high. Courtesy National Park Service, Bandelier National Monument.

Painted Cave

Painted Cave is about two and a half miles down Capulin Canyon from the site of Yapashi and its Stone Lions. Like Ceremonial Cave, this is actually a large recess beneath a rock overhang—a kind of geological feature that is relatively rare on the Pajarito Plateau. Painted Cave, too, opens toward the south. Cave rooms existed below the painted chamber when Adolph Bandelier first described it in 1880, but they have now largely eroded away.

Unlike much of the other ancient rock art on the plateau, the artwork here is painted (pictographs), rather than consisting of the more common engraved petroglyphs. Its many designs are often superimposed, but one can still make out the large, horned serpent, an image associated with the water gods, along with stars, kachina masks, stepped cloud designs, and human figures. Since the first photographs of Painted Cave were taken in the late 1800s, several pictographs have been added, suggesting that the site retains its sacred status.

Capulin Canyon is much dryer than Frijoles, and the landscape looks more like that of the Rio Grande Valley several miles to the east and five hundred feet lower in elevation. Judging from pottery found in Capulin Canyon, the area was relatively densely populated in the early to mid-1200s, the time when small pueblos and cliff houses were also constructed. But few intact ruins have been formally investigated here. Pottery fragments found near Painted Cave span the period from about 1150 to 1500, so it is difficult to tell just when the cave was painted. Judging from the style of the designs and the sequence in which they were painted over one another, many of the surviving paintings date between 1300 and 1600. At least one design was painted after Spaniards arrived in the area: it depicts a stylized human figure on horseback.

Pictographs in Painted Cave, in Capulin Canyon. Courtesy National Park Service, Bandelier National Monument.

Tsankawi

The ancient village of Tsankawi (see third plate) is in a detached, north-ern section of Bandelier Monument. It lies one and a half miles east of New Mexico Highway 4, where it forks toward Santa Fe. This northern area is rich in pueblo ruins, and Tsankawi is among the most spectacular.

Tsankawi's four large blocks of rooms are arranged in an irregular rectangle around a central plaza. The village consisted of 350 to 400 rooms and nearly a dozen kivas. Like other pueblos nearby, it was built of hand-cut volcanic tuff, mortared with adobe. Portions of Tsankawi once stood several stories high. Photographs taken a century ago show how the dete-rioration of such ruins has accelerated in modern times.

Tsankawi was one ancestral village of the modern-day Tewa speakers. Its name is contracted from a longer Tewa name, saekewikwaje onwikege, meaning "village between two canyons at the clump of sharp, round cac-tus." Deep trails worn into the Pajarito's soft, volcanic bedrock by many generations of Indian occupants still lead to the ruin. For visitors who have never seen such "foot-carved" trails, this ruin is worth the walk, which takes about two hours round-trip. Its mesa-top setting is impressive: cacti (mostly cholla) still grow there, along with sharp, narrow-leaf yucca, and from the ruin, one can see much of the surrounding mesa country. Like other late, Classic period pueblos on the plateau, Tsankawi lies in the piñon-juniper zone, in contrast to the higher ponderosa forest that people favored in the mid-1200s.

Tsankawi gave its name to a distinctive, Tewa-associated black-on-cream pottery. Although the site is not adequately dated, it flourished in the 1400s and 1500s. Like other Classic period pueblos established in the uplands, it likely functioned as a safety valve for Rio Grande popu-lations during times of drought, such as those of the 1420s, 1580s, and 1590s. Most of its farmland and the faint remains of one- and two-room field houses, typical of the Classic period, are in the canyon bottoms surrounding the Tsankawi mesa. People who farmed upland canyon bot-toms gained not only concentrated sources of water but also soils offering greater organic content.

Other Gifts from the Past

There are hundreds of other ruins to enjoy in Bandelier National Monument, but ancestral American Indian peoples gave the modern world much more than fascinating stone ruins. Some of today's food and clothing is also a legacy from the past. Native items that were common on the Pajarito and elsewhere in the Southwest, such as domesticated turkeys, corn, pinto and kidney beans, squash, tobacco, sunflower seeds, watermelons, and domesticated cotton, have all found their way into contemporary everyday lives. Corn, cotton, and their derivative products account for fully 20 percent of the U.S. agricultural economy. Visitors to Bandelier wearing cotton clothing and contemplating a summer meal of barbecued turkey, corn on the cob, baked beans, and watermelon are enjoying modern strains of horticultural products once carefully tended in tens of thousands of long-forgotten gardens. Ancient Indian America is much more than a tourist attraction; its accomplishments are the basis of many crucial sectors of our modern economy.

Resources

Akins, Nancy J.
1986   *A Biocultural Approach to Human Burials from Chaco Canyon, New Mexico.* Reports of the Chaco Center, no. 9. National Park Service, Santa Fe, New Mexico.

Akins, Nancy J., and John D. Schelberg
1984   "Evidence for Organizational Complexity as Seen from the Mortuary Practices at Chaco Canyon." In *Recent Research on Chaco Prehistory,* edited by W. James Judge and John D. Schelberg, pp. 89–102. Reports of the Chaco Center, no. 8. National Park Service, Albuquerque, New Mexico.

Bandelier, Adolph F.
1946   *The Delight Makers.* Dodd, Mead, New York.

Biella, Jan V., and Richard C. Chapman, editors
1977–79 *Archeological Investigations in Cochiti Reservoir, New Mexico.* 4 vols. Office of Contract Archaeology, University of New Mexico, Albuquerque.

Cordell, Linda S.
1980   *Tijeras Canyon: Analysis of the Past.* University of New Mexico Press, Albuquerque.
1997   *Archaeology of the Southwest.* 2nd edition. Academic Press, San Diego.

Doyel, David E., and Jeffrey S. Dean, editors
2006   *Environmental Change and Human Adaptation in the Ancient American Southwest.* University of Utah Press, Salt Lake City.

Dunmire, William W., and Gail D. Tierney
1995   *Wild Plants of the Pueblo Province.* Museum of New Mexico Press, Santa Fe.

Hoard, Dorothy
1983   *A Guide to Bandelier National Monument.* Los Alamos Historical Society, Los Alamos, New Mexico.

Jelinek, Arthur J.
1967   *A Prehistoric Sequence in the Middle Pecos Valley, New Mexico.* Anthropological Papers 31. Museum of Anthropology, University of Michigan, Ann Arbor.

Jennings, Jesse D., editor
1983   *Ancient North Americans.* W. H. Freeman, New York. See especially chapter 10, "The Southwest," by William D. Lipe, pp. 421–94.

Judge, James W.
1989   "Chaco Canyon—San Juan Basin." In *Dynamics of Southwest Prehistory*, edited by Linda S. Cordell and George J. Gumerman, pp. 209–62. Washington, DC: Smithsonian Institution Press. Reprint, Tuscaloosa: University of Alabama Press, 2006.

Kantner, John
2004   *Ancient Puebloan Southwest.* Cambridge University Press, Cambridge, U.K.

Kohler, Timothy A.
2004   *Archaeology of Bandelier National Monument: Village Formation on the Pajarito Plateau, New Mexico.* University of New Mexico Press, Albuquerque.

Lange, Charles H., and Carroll Riley
1966   *The Southwestern Journals of Adolph Bandelier, 1880–1882.* University of New Mexico Press, Albuquerque.

LeBlanc, Stephen
1996   *Prehistoric Warfare in the American Southwest.* University of Utah Press, Salt Lake City.

Lekson, Stephen H.
1986   *Great Pueblo Architecture of Chaco Canyon, New Mexico.* University of New Mexico Press, Albuquerque.
1999   *The Chaco Meridian,* AltaMira Press, Walnut Creek, California.

Ortiz, Alfonso, editor
1979   *Handbook of North American Indians,* vol. 9, *The Southwest.* Smithsonian Institution, Washington, DC.

Powers, Robert P., editor
2005   *The Peopling of Bandelier.* School for Advanced Research Press, Santa Fe, New Mexico.

Powers, Robert P., and Janet Orcutt, editors
1999   *The Bandelier Archaeological Survey.* 2 vols. National Park Service, Santa Fe, New Mexico.

Sebastian, Lynne
1992   *The Chaco Anasazi: Sociopolitical Evolution in the Prehistoric Southwest.* Cambridge University Press, Cambridge, U.K.

Stuart, David E.
1985   *Glimpses of the Ancient Southwest.* Ancient City Press, Santa Fe, New Mexico.
1985   "Prehistoric Pajarito." *New Mexico Magazine,* vol. 63, no. 1 (January), pp. 92–100.
2000   *Anasazi America.* University of New Mexico Press, Albuquerque.
2009   *The Ancient Southwest.* University of New Mexico Press, Albuquerque.

Stuart, David E., and Robin Farwell

1983   "Out of Phase: Late Pithouse Occupations in the Highlands of New Mexico." In *High Altitude Adaptations in the Southwest*, edited by Joseph C. Winter, pp. 115–50. USDA Forest Service, Southwest Region, Santa Fe, New Mexico.

Stuart, David E., and Rory P. Gauthier

1988   *Prehistoric New Mexico.* 2nd edition. University of New Mexico Press, Albuquerque.

Tainter, Joseph A., and D. A. Gilleo

1980   *Cultural Resources Overview: Mount Taylor Area, New Mexico.* USDA Forest Service and Bureau of Land Management, Albuquerque, New Mexico, and Washington, DC.

Traylor, Diane, Nancy Wood, Lyndi Hubbell, Robert Scaife, and Sue Weber

1977   "Bandelier Excavations in the Flood Pool of Cochiti Lake, New Mexico." Southwest Cultural Resources Center, National Park Service, Santa Fe, New Mexico.

Wills, W. H.

1988   *Early Prehistoric Agriculture in the American Southwest.* School of American Research Press, Santa Fe, New Mexico.

About the Author

DAVID E. STUART first came to New Mexico and to Bandelier National Monument in the winter of 1967–1968. After taking undergraduate studies in Mexico City, he completed his bachelor's degree at West Virginia Wesleyan College (1967) and earned a PhD in anthropology (1972) from the University of New Mexico (UNM). He taught college for several years in Florida before returning to UNM as a founding staff member of the Office of Contract Archaeology. L ater he entered academic administration at UNM. During the 1960s and 1970s, he conducted fieldwork in Alaska, Mexico, South America, the U.S. Southwest, and his native Appalachia. His biography appears in Who's Who in the West, Who's Who in America, and Who's Who in the World.

Stuart lives in Albuquerque, near UNM, where, although he is retired from his long-time post as associate provost for academic affairs, he still teaches the two-semester "Ancient New Mexico" sequence. His unusual approach to the Southwest combines anthropology, ecology, energetics, evolutionary theory, and archaeology as they pertain to both mistakes and triumphs in ancient times—in either case, compelling lessons for contemporary society. The author of twenty books, Stuart is an award-winning writer of archaeology, ethnographic nonfiction, and fiction who lectures often at the Southwest's national monuments and at European universities. He enjoys hearing from readers and can be contacted at AnasaziAmerica. com and at dstuart@unm.edu.